# STAGE
# IV
## ADDICTION

# STAGE
# IV
## ADDICTION

ADDICTED TO THE ADDICT

B.L. MARKS

authorHOUSE®

*AuthorHouse*™
*1663 Liberty Drive*
*Bloomington, IN 47403*
*www.authorhouse.com*
*Phone: 1 (800) 839-8640*

*Published by AuthorHouse 5/26/2015*

*ISBN: 978-1-5049-1241-9 (sc)*
*ISBN: 978-1-5049-1240-2 (e)*

*Library of Congress Control Number: 2015907745*

*Print information available on the last page.*

*Any people depicted in stock imagery provided by Thinkstock are models,*
*and such images are being used for illustrative purposes only.*
*Certain stock imagery © Thinkstock.*

*This book is printed on acid-free paper.*

*Because of the dynamic nature of the Internet, any web addresses or links contained in*
*this book may have changed since publication and may no longer be valid. The views*
*expressed in this work are solely those of the author and do not necessarily reflect the*
*views of the publisher, and the publisher hereby disclaims any responsibility for them.*

# Dancing With the Devil

I started writing this book after my son's death. I had known for many years that my son might die. It is a strange thing for a mother to say—that she knew her child's death was a possibility—but I did feel that way for quite some time. His disease had progressed so far that it was as if he was fighting the most malignant of all diseases.

My son had the disease of addiction. His drug of choice was heroin. After I tell my story, and his, you will better understand my reasons for "staging" this disease. Year after year, I watched my son battle with his addiction. As the years went on, the fact that this disease could take his life became my reality. You may wonder how someone would even find the drug. Trust me; it is not as difficult as you might think. I have so much to tell, and it is hard to know where to begin. However, every story is important. I hope this book will help me in my own recovery, recovery from the greatest tragedy of my life.

The first time I talked to my psychiatrist, he asked why I was there. I answered, "I'm addicted to the addict." I considered making the title of this book *Addicted to the Addict*, because that was my truth. I spent so much time trying to keep my son from killing himself. I have a lot of practice with addiction, and in this case, practice does not make perfect. I have to let myself believe that I did my best to save my son.

Writing this book has been a painful experience, to say the least. As far as stories go, this is not a happy one. As time goes on, I have flashbacks to situations that I had hidden in the back of my mind. Sometimes I wonder how I lived through it. Fear became such a mainstay in my life. How and why my son lived that life was my biggest question.

# AT FIRST GLANCE

My son was a wonderful human being. He was compassionate, well spoken, intelligent, talented, good-looking, and well loved. At least in sobriety, he was all of those things. Addiction stripped him of everything decent he thought he could be. I chose my words very carefully there: addiction stripped him of everything he thought he could be. I never lost faith in him. Through almost sixteen years of on-and-off hell, I remained in his corner.

Could I say that he was bright, talented, and compassionate when he was alive? No, not when he was using heroin. That would have been a tad hypocritical. I always said to my son, "You took my bragging rights away." People at work would brag about their children's talent, compassion, or whatever, and I would think to myself, *who is going to listen to the mother of a heroin addict?*

As they said in rehab, I was the enabler, and I was codependent. I was very resistant to that fact. I knew my son and knew that I could not turn my back on him. No one knew how to help him. They really did not know. Not when he started using, not the kid-next-door type of addict, and sadly, those were the ones who were hitting the streets.

# CAUTIONARY TALE

I make no claim to be an expert on addiction. That is not my intention at all. This is certainly not a book with advice about what to do if your child is an addict. If I could write such a book, my son would be alive today, and I would be a millionaire. A clear-cut idea of what stops some and not others is more valuable than life itself. Addiction is a nasty disease.

This is a cautionary tale. Judging by my experiences and the things I have seen and heard, the practices in rehabilitation centers in the late 1990s were a lot more archaic than they are now. Times have changed. I often wonder if my son would have benefited more if he were in treatment now. He always said to me, "Mom, I feel like I was born at the wrong time." I thought he meant he wanted to go back to the "good old days," the 1950s and 60s. He loved the music from that era and had a great appreciation for what seemed like a simpler lifestyle or maybe a simpler society.

When we talked about the future and I would say, "When you are forty …" he would interject, "I won't be alive when I'm forty."

I always responded, "Please, don't say that." I never asked him why he said that. I knew why. He knew why. Call me crazy, but I believe he had an old soul.

# HOOKED

I have had so many insights, awakenings, and realizations since my son's death. Many publicized incidents of addiction have taken place, both locally and nationwide. It is obvious that society sees this problem from a different point of view. That is because it is hitting home. People have become more aware that addiction is more common than was originally understood. This is not a new problem and it is only because it has hit the middle class that addiction is becoming such a hot topic. We didn't care so much when it stayed in the ghetto. The "professionals" also have finally figured out that mental-health issues are a big factor. It may not be so everywhere, but in our state heroin addiction has exploded.

New laws have been passed in the state. They require doctors to log on to a special website when prescribing any narcotic. When the doctor logs on, he or she is able to review every prescription a patient has been given—how often it has been filled, how many pills were dispensed, the prescribing doctor's and Pharmacy's information. Doctors now have enough information to determine if there is a problem; in other words, they can tell if you are "hooked." Drug seeking is what they called it. Typically, the doctor will decide to stop giving the patient those meds. The patient may decide to get some help and stop, or he may take to the streets. This is why heroin has the great opportunity to become an epidemic. Drug pushers are selling narcotics on the street—Xanax, hydros, oxys, just about any drug you want, is out there for a price. The pharmaceutical narcotics are sold on the street for big bucks, but thankfully, fewer and fewer are available. That is progress. However, heroin is still out there, and it is cheap.

That made front-page news: people are resorting to heroin because it is cheap and easier to get. That is a very scary thought. My son always seemed to relapse on hydrocodone. People have a misconception that pharmaceuticals are the lesser of the evils. Wrong! In case you do not know, and many people do not, hydrocodone is an opiate derivative, and opiates are highly addictive. It doesn't take much and it doesn't take long. I heard a young female addict describe the first time she took heroin as it feeling like a warm hug. SCARY.

# THE DAY I FOUND OUT

It was a Saturday morning. I was wallpapering our kitchen, and I remember it like it was yesterday. I got a phone call from my son's best friend. My son was at work.

He said, "Mom, what are you doing?" I told him I was wallpapering the kitchen.

"Can I come over and talk with you?" he asked. "I have something to discuss with you."

I sensed the seriousness in his tone, and knew there had to be some kind of big problem concerning my son. I do not know why, but the next words out of my mouth were, "You're not going to tell me that he is using heroin, are you?" There had been talk amongst his friends regarding the fact that heroin was going around. Never did I picture my son using it.

He did not answer my question. He just said, "I need to come and speak with you." I had begun to know that my son was changing and that there was something going on. I admit I could not put my finger on it. I really could not tell if it was a good or a bad change, to be perfectly honest with you. My son had become amazingly calm around that time. I guess they call that a mother's instinct. Go with your gut. Something did feel different.

My son's friend arrived at my house. He sat me down and told me that my son was on heroin, and could not stop. His friend told me that my son's using had become more than just a problem; it was consuming him.

I had at this point called my son at work and asked him to come home. I did not tell him why. I just told him it was an emergency.

At that point, my son ran in with a look of sheer panic.

His friend told him, "Look, I told your mom about your heroin problem and that we are all very worried about you. We know you're not able to stop, and we think you need to get some help."

I had no idea his friends were this concerned. It must have become really bad for his friend to come to me.

I also knew nothing about rehabs or detox. I was unaware that heroin was so out of control in our area. I had no idea how prevalent it had become in our neck of the woods. I had only seen it in movies. I did not realize that it had infiltrated our society as much as it had. This could not be happening to my son. Why my son? He had so much to offer. He was so bright, talented, and loving. It was beyond me how this could happen to him, but it did.

# DETOX

My son then told me that he needed to go to detox.

I asked, "What is detox?"

He explained it was "a hospital facility where I can go for four to five days. They will watch and help me get through withdrawal symptoms."

Withdrawal symptoms? What withdrawal symptoms? I called his father and told him to come home as soon as possible; it was an emergency. The two of us took our son to detox that afternoon.

My son said there was a detox facility at a hospital downtown. We had no idea what we were dealing with. I called, and they said they had a bed available and to bring him in. They asked if he was actively using. What? Yes he was, I answered.

On the fifth day, we picked him up from the detox facility and took him home. He was adamant that he did not want to use anymore. We thought that would be our experience with our son's addiction. He did not want to use anymore; we thought it was as simple as that.

Boy, were we surprised when we found out he was using again. It seemed as soon as we learned about his addiction, the worse it got. I did not realize back then that this could be a progressive disease.

# Meetings and Rehab

I went to meetings with him, but they did not work because he would run into the most despicable characters. My son was a very nice-looking young man, and every time we went to a meeting, he became a target for some unsavory person with ill intentions. There also was a certain amount of competition between the addicts: who had it worse? My son and I sat there and listened. They always seemed to be telling war stories, to be telling stories of their glory days. I would walk out confused. It certainly did not seem like a life of glory to me. Remember back then my son's type added a new landscape to the mix. Remember this was around 1997.

When he relapsed again, we took him to a facility downstate. A friend of my husband had recommended it. This man said that this facility had helped him deal with his alcoholism. My son could go there because he was still considered a student, and was young enough to be covered on his father's insurance. I drove him to the facility, which was about two-and-a-half hours away. I think it was a twenty-eight-day program. I expected to see a man show his face at the door and say, "Here's Johnny." The place just gave you that feeling. It was scary and gothic-looking. Twenty-eight days later, I went to pick him up.

Good God, he was convincing. He was "never going to use again"; this place really got to him. My son insisted that he absolutely wanted to remain clean and did not want to use heroin anymore. When he said that, he wanted it to be true. Stupid me, I knew so little about addiction. I did not realize that just because he wanted to stop did not mean the demon had stopped calling his name. My son was heavily addicted.

I cannot remember how long we kept him under our wing to make sure he did not get into trouble. I can probably say this is where my super-vigilance started.

He relapsed again. I took him to another twenty-eight-day program. Again, I thought this would work, since he insisted he really wanted to stop. This rehab had a family day. It was led by a young woman who got up on a podium and addressed an auditorium of addicts and their families. She introduced herself as Nancy; she was a nurse, and she came from a long line of addicts, mostly alcoholics. She herself was a recovering alcoholic. She made it clear to us that this was a genetic thing. If she had brothers, a father, and a grandfather who were alcoholics and she was a recovering one, it had to be genetic or learned behavior.

"Everyone here who is in the medical field, raise your hands," Nancy said to the crowd. I am a nurse, so I hesitantly raised my hand and noticed that others did the same.

She looked at all of us and said, "Okay, well, you people are screwed because you think that you can fix everything, and that is not going to happen in this case."

I was shocked, and yet I knew she was right. I could not fix this on my own just because I wanted it to be gone.

My son did his twenty-eight-day stint at the facility. Most of the counselors were recovering addicts; that is usually the case at rehab centers. I realize now that they were not prepared to deal with his mental-health issues. I am sure their intentions were good, but no two ways about it, my son was a die-hard addict. That is always the term I use to describe him. During the next sixteen years of his life, and mine, I would learn that there is a lot more to drug addiction. I learned all my lessons, and so did he—the hard way.

I do not remember how long my son stayed clean or at what point he relapsed, but he did relapse.

# ANGER

My conversations with my son were serious and in-depth, but only when we were alone. His father would become quite irate and had very little compassion for the fact that our son had a disease. He believed my son was being self-indulgent, that he was paying us back for the wrong things we had done as young parents. My husband was very angry about our son's addiction, and he had no filter at all; he just said what he felt. I always found this quite confusing because who else but another addict could understand an addict better? I had felt that my husband had problems with alcohol for a long time. He really could not equate the two as being similar.

# THE NEWLYWEDS

Our son was born when I was twenty-five years old and my husband was twenty-three. We were kids ourselves. My husband was never too involved in the parenting of our son. He pretty much did his own thing and sowed some wild oats with his friends.

I had to settle down because I was now a mom. I became pregnant with my daughter in 1983 when my son was six years old. He was thrilled to be a big brother; he loved her to death, and even though they were six years part, they looked a lot alike.

Fortunately, or unfortunately, my husband got his first full-time job. He became a liquor salesman. I soon found out that this business not only was very unhealthy for us as a family, but it also exacerbated my husband's own addiction. My husband had his own demons, and he always was the reactive type. If you pushed his buttons, he would overreact and never considered the consequences of his outbursts.

My son later wrote, "I realized that my father drank a little too much." He was being very kind. (For more of my son's writing, see the chapter titled "Jail 2009.") That really was an understatement. My life turned upside down. I had two children and no husband. My husband was young, good-looking, and very personable. The life of a liquor sales representative suited him just fine. I tried to keep my mouth shut. I never was much of a complainer, I had made my own choices, and now I had to live with them. You may say I was a wimp. I should have stood my ground and left, but I felt I needed to keep trying. I came from a generation where marriage was supposed to be forever. I never wanted to give up, so I tried to love him unconditionally.

There certainly was a time when I felt alone and that I was in the middle of a nightmare. I would try to reason with my husband and make him realize how painful it was for me and that he was risking his life, our children's lives, and my life. There was no talking to him when he was drunk. The next morning he always expressed regrets, and said he would tone it down and be more responsible. Sound like anybody you know?

How could he drive like that? It scared the shit out of me. His whole demeanor changed when he was drunk. He was a nasty drunk. I never complained to my family or his about the situation. I always thought they would say, "Well, you got married too young." I believed I had to suck it up. My feelings of loneliness went on for years and years. We had a very large group of friends back then and, to be honest, they all drank too much. I knew I would not find too much comfort discussing this with them.

As time went on, I started to hate my husband. The more I asked him not to drink, the more he drank. He worked for a company that did not see drinking as a problem. Many of his coworkers also drank too much. It was part of the job. I realized it had become a problem. We often discussed this, and it always caused a lot of fighting and screaming and the same response from him: "I am not an alcoholic."

He did not drink every single day, but when he drank, he drank too much. He became so different from the person I had first met. At times, I was frightened. I did not know this person and was never quite sure how far he would go when he was drunk. I did not have the slightest idea of what to do. *Leave him? Stay? How could I convince him he had a problem?*

Better yet, how could I convince him that I had a problem with his problem? I had questions, but no answers. You see, this is where my guilt comes in. When I found out my son was a heroin addict, I often thought back to this time in our lives.

Sometimes I overcompensated with the kids. I did not know how to handle my husband's problem, our problem. He was never going to agree that he drank too much. He was not going to get any help because he did not think he needed it. That is part of the disease. God knows, I needed help.

I was more than neglected and hurt by his life without me. When we were dating, we always did things together. Now we were living our lives without each other, and he did not mind. That was not a great example for my son. My daughter was only three at the time and was not as privy as my son was to our yelling and screaming.

Before his dad walked in the door, my son would say, "Mom, please don't say anything to him." He was very frightened by my confrontations with his father, who was very arrogant and aggressive when he had been drinking.

I tried to be the best mom I could be, and my son always told me that I was a good mom.

As the years went on, my husband's drinking became worse. Lord knows, I could not keep up with him. It made me sick as a dog, and I did stupid things when I was drunk. That had to stop.

Yes, we smoked pot. My husband and I often had heated discussions about it. I did not stick to my guns, which was immature on my part. One of my many regrets about that time in my life is that I did not have much of a backbone. I should have left. Indeed, a counselor said to me one day, "Why the hell didn't you just leave him? Nobody would've blamed you."

This was my big mistake, to be honest. Given the choice of having him either stoned or drunk, I would have pick stoned any day. All our friends smoked pot. It seemed to be the lesser of the evils. He was much more mellow and easier to tolerate when he was stoned. I let him smoke openly, which was a bad choice.

# OUR FIRST HOUSE

We moved into a house built by my husband and his father. Previously we'd lived in a duplex and had become friendly with the couple next door. I always liked the couple very much. I talked to the man as we both mowed the lawn. He was funny, kind, and an all-around great person. He helped us move into our new house, and we all remained friends after the move. We remained closer to him than with his wife after we moved. Although I liked his wife too, we never became fast friends.

I worked part-time nights at a hospital, which meant I was often home during the day. One February morning, it was snowing out, and the phone rang. It was our neighbor. Although we were all friends, I always thought that because he was a man, he was more my husband's friend than mine. That did not turn out to be true. He became my best friend.

In our first conversation, I said, "My husband is not here."

"I didn't call to speak to him," he said. "I called to speak to you. How are you?"

That was all I needed—someone calling to find out how I was. Our relationship took off from there. He called often, and we would talk. He filled a gaping void in my life. He was an awesome person, and I loved him dearly. My husband could tell that I had started to care less and less about his bad behavior; I think that was more of a giveaway than anything else. For the first time in my ten-year marriage, I saw myself as separate from my husband.

The laws were much different back then. Now, if you drove as drunk as he used to, they would throw you in prison and probably throw away the key. The more I argued with him about his drinking, the more he drank. I really did not care what my husband did anymore.

I just filled the void with my male friend. At that time, and being as stupid as I was, that was the only defense mechanism I had, considering I was too chicken to address my husband's continued drinking.

All of our friends probably would have thought it very unlikely for me to be the one to have a long, ongoing affair. In my mind, I did not consider it an affair. I actually considered it a relationship and really thought we would be together. Our affair lasted four years before my husband figured it out. Once the relationship was discovered I could not find it in my heart to continue and rip our two families apart. That relationship was one of the most irresponsible things I have ever done.

# BIRDS OF A FEATHER

Naturally, when my son's addiction problem started six years later, I wondered whether my husband and I were to blame. I never had a good answer for my bad behavior. My husband and I worked on our relationship. It was not easy through the years, but I was willing to do this because of the kids. I knew that no matter how bad our behavior was, our son idolized his father as did our daughter, and neither one wanted our relationship to be broken. I guess I have always had the guilt thing; maybe going to parochial school made it come to me more naturally.

My son continued to go in and out of rehab. Eventually it became too much to explain to people. Then he started having multiple legal issues. My son was constantly being arrested.

I do not want to give the impression that my son was alone through his addiction. He often came out of a program with a girlfriend. One time he came out of a nine-month, court- mandated program with a young woman I absolutely idolized. She was one of his counselors. It was totally against the rules, but they had a five-year relationship. When she talked to him in the program, he was clean and sober, and he had a sensitivity that was beyond reproach. How could you not fall in love with this beautiful, loving young man? She saw him through so much, and sat around with me for hours on end, waiting for him to come home. I do not know how she did it. She truly was my best friend and confidant at that time.

He loved her very much. In addition, he idolized her family—her mother, father, grandmother, grandfather, aunts and uncles. He stole from them too, and he could never forgive himself, even when they forgave him. She and my son remained friends till the end. They would talk on and off, and she admitted feeling guilty after his death, wishing that she had returned more of his phone calls. He always worried about her when he did not speak to her. He thought there was something she did not want to share. She had been there for him, but she was going through her own stuff. She referred to him as a "lovable pain in the ass." I mention her because she was such an integral part of my son's life and mine. I remember her with great fondness and love, and my love, prayers, and good thoughts will always be with her.

# THE BOY NEXT DOOR

My son was always such a happy child. I never would have thought that depression would become his problem, but I realize now that depression is inevitable when you live the life of an addict. That he was anesthetizing himself from depression or anxiety never occurred to me. Now I believe that anxiety is what got him hooked on heroin.

I am a nurse in a medical office, and not long ago I got a call from a patient. We had spoken before. She had heard about my son's passing and asked me if there were one thing I could do over again with my son, one thing I could change, what it would be. It did not take me any time at all to answer her. I said, "I would have delved a lot deeper into his mental-health issues."

My son probably suffered from mental-health issues throughout his addiction, but I lost sight of that when I was trying everything to keep him sober and alive. It is not the first thing you think about in the beginning. The fact that my son was destined to live this struggle is something I will never understand. No one would deliberately choose this life because it is not a life at all. An addict is not living.

As I mentioned earlier, my son was very handsome. When he was sober, he looked like Dapper Dan, but when he was using he often dressed down. It was almost like he had a part in a play. He could not be a heroin addict without looking like a heroin addict. I asked myself a million times why a person who cared so much about how he looked and what people thought about him made himself look like such a piece of shit.

He was not famous. He was just a normal kid who, unfortunately, found his drug of choice and got hooked. I really do believe that some people are lucky enough not to find their drug of choice.

I have been told by recovered addicts that my son often told new junkies, "Hey man, you really don't want to walk this path," and they took his advice. He told them some scary stories.

We never had any problems with my son as a child, although he was a wanderer. He was smart, very compassionate, personable, and lovable. Everyone loved him. There was nothing not to love.

My mom and dad had two girls, so he was the first boy in the family, and they idolized him. I remember his first day at grammar school; he was six years old and as cool as a cucumber. I have a picture of him on that first day, leaning up against the tree in the front yard, waiting for the school bus. He always appeared to be equipped for what life would throw at him. Boy was I wrong about that.

# The Good Old Days

Looking back at my own childhood, I realize I knew many people with addictions. However, *addiction* was not the term people used back then. That word was set aside for the "street urchins" who were using heroin or for people lying in a drunken stupor in an alley somewhere. We used to think that these people had overindulged and had weaknesses or did not know how to control themselves. No one ever addressed these problems.

Drugs, cigarettes, booze, gambling, sex, overeating—these were all problems that I witnessed in my own family, but I never thought of them as addictions. I also never thought of them as genetic. After watching my son and seeing the things I have seen, I believe you can be born with a gene that makes you prone to that weakness. That is scary.

Oh, and let us not forget about gambling. There are those who can tell you about losing everything to a bad gambling habit, but wait—is it just a bad habit? No, it is an addiction. Coming out of the closet about the fact you are an addict seems self-deprecating, until you lose it all. That is when you are thrown out of the closet and the jig is up.

I was in the car recently and heard a radio advertisement for a bariatric surgeon. The commercial referred to obesity as a disease. Some people will say that obese people choose to overeat and overindulge; all they have to do is stop eating and control their eating habits.

Why do some things seem so simple for some people? Obesity is a disease. For some people, food is their drug of choice; it fills a void and gives them comfort.

When people suffer from unwanted side effects and repercussions, whether due to food, drugs, booze, cigarettes, sex, or gambling, they become addicted.

I have seen people ruin their minds, lose their loved ones, and die because of addiction. The biggest and most important thing they lose is their self-respect—a major loss!

Please do not get me wrong. Recovery is attainable. They used to say that the addict had three choices—recovery, jail, or death. My son experienced all three.

# THE GENE

Let us talk about the gene of addiction. I am not the first person to say that addiction is inherited. I firmly believe that is true and support those who agree.

There is a gene that predisposes an individual to become an addict. I have an addiction to cigarettes. It is not a matter of if they will kill me; it is a matter of when.

I have watched addiction happen to many families, including my own and my husband's, for many years. When I was growing up in the 1960s and 70s, experimentation with drugs was the thing to do. It seemed everybody was experimenting. It seemed that many had their drug of choice.

I was also aware that many of my good friends—people who seemed sensible, bright, and rational—were moving ahead with their experimentation. Some of them became addicted, and some were able to stop. Some people just have a glitch in their brain that leads them to become addicts. That gene.

Yes, I smoked pot, but I never felt it was something I had to have. I still stand my ground and maintain that I do not feel pot is a gateway drug.

Even the authorities—meaning rehab, courts, outpatient care, lawyers, etc.—were ill prepared for a case like my sons. They did not understand his mental-health issues. I myself did not realize that after a while mental health plays a crucial part in them remaining addicts. I do not think anybody knew what to do with him. Remember this was in the late 90's. He truly was like the kids next door.

He was in stage 1 addiction long before we even knew he had a problem. It is when it became a full-time job. Taking heroin every day to maintain a feeling of wellbeing. My son would tell me that there were times when he used so that he didn't remember the good times. That is sad. That is stage 2.

He was very active as a child, but he was not hyperactive. He definitely wanted to please people, and that is where the story becomes a contradiction or maybe not. I truly have learned that people pleasing is not always healthy. Hindsight is twenty/twenty—no two ways about it. I look back now and see all the signs and signals and wonder what I could have done differently.

He had periods of sobriety. Whether he had been in rehab, court-mandated shock incarceration, probation or jail. His sobriety never seemed to last too long.

# STAGES

I will not win any friends by saying that I believe addiction happens in stages. We have stages for cancer, and after watching my son's struggle, I believe there are stages to the disease of addiction.

Remember, I had a front-row seat, watching this kid battle his addiction. I did not walk away from him, and that was definitely my own choice. Many people could not deal with his addiction so they walked away. I have known other people I should have walked away from, but I stood by them. I could not turn my back on my son.

I cannot tell you how many times I told myself he would have had an easier time if he were going through cancer treatment. They recover or go into remission, but they can never be 100 percent certain that they will not relapse. Both diseases can be fatal. The difference between the cancer patient and the addict is that when they do relapse, nobody calls the cancer sufferer a scumbag. No one turns his back on cancer patients. Doctors rally around them, and the medical team tries every means to come up with a treatment or cure.

The phrase "relapse is part of the disease" was very common when my son was first starting treatment. Relapse can occur with both cancer and addiction. I grew very tired of hearing that phrase. Believe me I get it: relapse is part of the disease.

# STAGE 1 ADDICTION

At the beginning of my son's addiction, before we were aware that he was an addict, he was still in a functional state. One afternoon, I was sitting in our living room; he had just arrived home from college. He went to a local college, so he came home often. I remember it like it was yesterday. He looked so calm and so together.

"I am so proud of you," I said. "You have really calmed down and learned how to carry yourself like an adult."

When I remember that day, I realize what a fool I was. He looked cool, calm, and collected because he was a functional heroin addict. I often wonder what he thought when I said that. Yes, you can be functional in the beginning of addiction. It fools you and makes you think that it is working with you and for you. Over- time it consumes you.

To my surprise, he remembered what I said and wrote about it (see the chapter titled "Jail 2009"). As the years went by, his addiction escalated to a point where it became disabling. I have no better way to explain it. People tend to think that addiction is a bad choice, made by bad people, but nice people become addicts too. It is sad but true.

# THE FACE OF ADDICTION

I started this book and then stopped, started again and stopped multiple times. I worry about forgetting something that needs to be said. There are experiences I need to share. I am not sure that writing this will be a cleansing mechanism for me. However, I can say that losing my son has been devastating. This is truly a raw type of pain. I constantly tell myself not to dwell. Naturally while writing this it becomes all consuming. Again, my choice. I do not want to suggest I have no fond memories of my son because that is not true.

My son always wanted to help the underdog, the hurt and downtrodden; that was second nature to him. He was very compassionate person and the first one to help a person lying in the street. The using child was not the child I raised and certainly not the person he wanted to be. He had no sensibility at all when he was detoxing.

Let me give an example of something that happened early in his addiction. This indicates how desperate the person has to be when he starts jonesing for that drug. He went to a very large, crowded mall one afternoon and came upon a kiosk. My son saw that the salesperson had the register open, and although he was surrounded by customers, he put his hand in the register, grabbed the money, and ran. Naturally, he was arrested taken to the police station and charged. It was one of many court dates.

When I became aware of this incident, I knew we had one hell of a problem on our hands. Who does that kind of thing? A crazy person? That is how desperate he was. Please remember I felt I knew this person well and this was to me a very out of character move for him.

I used to picture a big brown blob, of I don't know, I guess probably shit, walking to my son's bedroom door and waking him up every morning saying, "Hey, come on, let's go. We have to get our fix."

Addiction is a disease! I will not back down from that statement. My son took his own life on January 6, 2012. The note he left read, "Please don't let my life be for nothing." Not only did he struggle with addiction, he committed suicide. I often wonder why my son became the poster child for addiction and then suicide.

Through the years of his addition, my son did horrible things. He stole from everybody he loved. Believe me when I say that some of the side effects of this disease are lying, stealing, and manipulation.

If an addict does not possess good coping skills, his sober moments can really do a job on him. Guilt was a heavy burden for my son. In fact, I truly believe that sobriety was painful for him. People may find that statement confusing, but it was a fact. He would relapse, recover, gather some coping skills, and take six steps forward, then ten steps back. Each time he relapsed, he picked up more and more baggage. Is being unable to forgive yourself a shortcoming? It was for him.

# CELEBRATE

Then there were three years of wonderful sobriety with a young woman he loved very much, and his life was golden. No one, not even my son, thought that he would risk what he had. All he had gained, all the friends he had, a girl he adored. However, as they always say in rehab: relapse is part of the disease.

I cringed the first time I heard that from a counselor and thought, *Oh my God, don't say that. How can you say that relapse is part of the disease?* It felt like a prophecy to me. It turned my stomach.

# LET THEM HIT ROCK BOTTOM

Another phrase counselors said constantly was that the addict "had to hit rock-bottom." As my son's disease progressed, I did not know how much more rockbottom he could hit without dying. Many times I thought he was at rock-bottom, that it couldn't get any worse, and that somewhere along the line it just had to stop because he would be so disgusted with his life as an addict but he was a die-hard addict; there is no other way to describe him.

"Tough love" was another expression counselors used. "Kick them out of the house" was yet another. A number of expressions in this book may not be familiar to readers. Some of them I probably made up based on sixteen years of experience living with an addict. For example, I use the term "running partner," which is the person an addict takes up with; he usually is in the same predicament as the addict, and they help each other on a daily basis to get their facts and finances in order to survive. It is a day-to-day survival game for addicts. From the moment they get up in the morning to the time they go to bed at night, their job is to make sure they have enough dope for the day to feel well, to forget, to survive.

"Falling out," a term used in the drug world, means that someone has overdosed or appears to have overdosed; it means respiratory arrest. Addicts end up in a semiconscious state. If that happens when a group of dope addicts is around, half of them would just as soon dump the person in the street rather than call an ambulance. When one addict falls out, it is as if a panic button is pushed for the others. Naturally, it is very hard to keep your wits about you when you are so doped up.

My son made many trips to the emergency room. Medical professionals allow addicts who are on the brink of destruction to walk out of the emergency room. One might wonder how that can happen. The doctors let them go, knowing that falling out is a frequent occurrence, that they are literally killing themselves. It makes me wonder where the responsibilities of the medical and legal professions begin and end.

# SOBRIETY

When my son was sober, he was creative and had a stunning sense of humor. He was good-looking, intelligent, and could put words together better than anybody. He was one of the most talented people I have ever known. He sang and wrote some beautiful music. I visited his apartment one afternoon, and there was music playing.

I asked, "Who are we were listening to?"

He laughed and said, "It's me, Mom." I was shocked. I had never heard him singing on tape. He was awesome.

As I stated earlier, he'd always gravitated to the underdog, and then this disease turned him into the underdog. He became everything he hated—a liar, a thief, and a criminal who could lie with the best of them. Even as a child, he could carry on a conversation with an adult. He was charismatic. He told me, maybe six years into his disease, that he took all his charisma and used it to do bad things. He often said he felt guilty about that.

# INSANITY

I always knew my son to be a loving young man. Please be aware that addiction can change the person you once knew. It took me a lot of time to realize that when he was using he was not the son I remembered. He never did things halfway. It was all or nothing; there were no gray areas. They used to say in rehab, "The definition of insanity is doing the same thing over and over again and thinking that you're going to have a different outcome."

Was he insane? There were moments when I questioned my own sanity. The biggest question was, does addiction make you crazy? I think it eventually does. How could somebody so bright and intelligent think that he would come out on the other end of this thing with anything tangible, worthwhile, worth living for? He believed he was doomed.

# MENTAL HEALTH

As mentioned above, mental-health issues were not addressed in rehabilitation centers during the 1990s. Patients would be there for about twenty-eight days, if they were lucky enough to have insurance. Then they would be released to an outpatient program. Most of the counselors were not prepared to handle the complexities that took place in the addicts' minds.

The counselors explained the legalities and the baggage that addicts picked up while they were using. They said addicts had three choices—recovery, jail, or death. My son used to call rehab a "quick rinse and spin." I understand that statement. I do not think I had the wisdom or courage to admit that he had a mental illness. Today, self-medication seems more popular than ever. Even if the addict does not seem to have a mental illness, it does not take a psychiatrist to see mental-health issues as his or her addiction progresses.

It is like the age-old question: what came first, the chicken or the egg? If there are mental-health issues in the beginning, the addiction exacerbates those issues, and addicts become completely rewired. Their brain chemistry goes way off. I have watched programs that showed MRIs of the brains of addicts and non-addicts. The difference between the two is astonishing. Hot spots in the addict's brain stand out like big red pools of cancer.

# SHORTCOMINGS

Self-assessment was one of the horrible side effects that I acquired with my son's disease. I would look back on the stupid things that his father and I had done. I would tell myself that none of it was so terrible that we deserve to have our beautiful son become a heroin addict. As a parent, you often wonder if your stupidity influences your child's behavior. *Was he too sensitive? Was he too compassionate? Did he fake compassion even when he did not feel it?* These are all questions I asked myself. I was constantly scrutinizing myself to determine what I could have done differently. The past is the past, however. There was nothing I could do to change his bad behavior. That was the reality.

He had a sister who was watching all of this. Looking back on the turmoil, I now realize that she must have felt the safety of her home was compromised.

# HAPPY BIRTHDAY TO ME

It was February 17, 1999—my birthday. I was at work and received a phone call from the police station. They had already had many dealings with my son, and even they had a hard time understanding how he had gotten himself into such a mess. They had picked him up for shoplifting, and they wanted me to pick up his belongings. I left work in a hurry to go down to the police station. I also wanted to go home because my daughter had a couple of friends coming over, and she was fixing dinner for me. I did not want to disappoint her because she was going through so much effort to put the dinner together.

At the police station, I was taken to the back of the squad room. My son sat there with a young police officer, crying with snot running down his face. He had his guitar with him. On a chair nearby was a plant he had bought for my birthday. It had a small balloon that said, "Happy Birthday, Mom." After my son bought the plant, he did not have enough money to buy cigarettes, so he stole the cigarettes and put them in his pocket. This was back in the day when cigarettes were on a rack at the checkout counter. He was caught on camera and when the police arrived at the supermarket, they frisked him and found syringes tucked into his jeans. That was when I learned that when he wanted to hide his syringes, he would make a little slit on the inside band at the top of his jeans and slip them there.

He had a needle-exchange card in his wallet. The police officer was very interested in the card and called the number on it. The person on the other end of the line told the officer, "Sir, this is a private needle-exchange program to keep these kids from using dirty needles. I can't divulge any information to you, and that is the law." I did not even know there was a needle-exchange program.

Now they had him for shoplifting and carrying paraphernalia. On my birthday, I was walking out of a police station carrying the plant and my son's guitar. Not for the first time, I called my son the wandering minstrel.

My daughter was making spaghetti and meatballs. I came home without her brother; no words were said but she knew. Sadly, this became a commonplace occurrence in our home.

Through these hard times, my daughter continued to be the achiever. She was the theater geek, the chorus geek. I was always very proud of her and her strength. Even with all the chaos around her, she remained strong. When he was clean, my son and his sister spent a lot of time together. They enjoyed each other's company immensely. I know she loved him, and there was never a question about his love for her.

He was a smart boy, but this drug turned him into a moron. He never thought logically when he was using. I learned early on that this drug had him by the balls. How do I know this? He did the most unbelievable things, took some of the most unbelievable chances, and suffered some of the worst consequences that I have ever seen.

# More Common than Ever

Addiction is all around us. An addict could be the person who works next to you in the office, the person standing next to you in the grocery store. Some of the most unlikely people in the world are addicts. People would never be able to point them out in a crowd.

My parents' generation all seemed to be cigarette smokers and alcohol drinkers. Parties, holidays, and family gatherings always included smoking and drinking, and it seemed to be the norm. Sure, people got drunk on those occasions, should not have been driving, and yes, they had problems. There were consequences, but society did not really address them. I saw many alcoholics lose everything, but the understanding of this as a disease was not there. Please do not lose sight that alcohol is a drug. Only those who went to meetings back then realized they were battling with the consequences of their addiction. Unfortunately, these types of meetings were closeted at that time, primarily to protect the anonymity of the attendees.

People were embarrassed to say that they went to meetings. There always seemed to be great shame in admitting that you had an addiction problem. The public was not aware of their battles. Now I realize that any addiction can snuff you out like a match.

We tend to be a very judgmental society. We set people in categories, such as "successful" or "unsuccessful." We need to become more compassionate and sensitive to those around us.

There are all kinds of outreach groups; the problem is that you have to realize you need one and not feel shame in searching for one and asking for help. I have gotten to the point in my life that I have more respect for the person who tells me they are a recovering addict than I do for the person who is in denial. That is learned behavior on my part because I never thought about the issue or thought I would have to deal with it. Boy did I learn how to deal with it.

# COPING SKILLS

Coping seems to be an important word when talking about this disease. Remember the word. *Coping.* As his addiction passed through the various stages, my son's coping skills depleted. Whenever he got out of rehab, he was clean and seemed to be back to his old, sober self. There was always something missing. The difference between when he was clean and when he was using was like night and day. After years of addiction and multiple programs, however, you could tell that he was not prepared for what he would face in the outside world. He was clean; now what? No one really prepares you for life after addiction. That always remained a big problem for him.

The addiction world is quite different from the world most people live in every day. At the rate things are going, I do not know how society will take care of the epidemic that has ensued. All I can do is appeal to those who are using opiates or any other kind of drug: please do not! You will lose all sense of self. You not only will lose material things but also dignity, self-respect, the ability to face reality, and the ability just to live a normal life. Once you get into addiction, you no longer live a normal life. You will lose control. You will experience things that nightmares are made of.

Any young person who thinks that drugs will solve his or her problems is very sadly mistaken. Drugs will exacerbate your problems so badly that you will regret you ever tried them. I know my son did. In fact, when he was clean, he inspired a few addicts to stay clean, saying, "Don't get into this shit, man. It will take you down." Yes, it will.

# THOSE POOR ADDICTS

I am fully aware that some people will take offense to my reference to those poor addicts. Please remember people do not start using drugs with the goal of becoming an addict. It is not fun.

Not long ago a popular young man died of a heroin overdose. A reporter on one of the entertainment channels reported on his premature death. She talked about his death with much legitimate sadness, but she let something slip. She said, "He seemed like such a nice young man ..." Yeah, well, guess what? He *was* a nice young man—a nice young man with an addiction problem.

A well-known actor made a plea to his audience as he stood at a podium. He said, "We have to do something about this drug-addiction thing. We are losing too many talented performers." Are you kidding me? We are losing too many of our sons and daughters. I was so incensed when I heard those comments. I have watched people, especially my own son, struggle for years. Does it have to hit you in the face before you realize that this can happen to someone you love?

Visiting rehabs was something to which I became very accustomed. My son had been in and out of so many programs that it soon became obvious that a person has to want to be clean. Rehab seems to be a cooling-off period for some.

There is a phrase addicts use: "You can talk the talk, but you have to walk the walk." Even famous people with tons of money come out of rehab programs and relapse repeatedly. They can afford these programs and still have problems recovering from their addictions. Some of them slip into stage 4 addiction. They forget they have to take care of the mental-health issues.

In my opinion, an addict will always need to consider him or herself an addict. There is a commercial in which a young man who runs a rehab facility states, "This is not a twelve-step program. I was an addict for ten years, and I'm not anymore." Really? I don't think you can shuffle that important part of a lifetime aside and pretend it didn't happen. Living the life of an addict for ten years is major.

My husband and my family have had our share of family drunks. Nobody knew why people drank so much. It never seemed to be addressed. It was just something they did. Why? Were they also self-anesthetizing? Watching the family drunk was painful for me when I was a child. My aunt drank too much. It was quite an issue for my beautiful cousin. I remember a conversation between her and my uncle; it must have been 1970.

She said, "Hey, Dad, you have to do something about her."

"And what would you like me to do about her?" asked my uncle.

My cousin answered, "I really don't know, but you have to put her someplace."

My poor cousin was always upset about her moms' drinking. It was a problem, and there was no place to go. There were no facilities back then. My aunt was never going to tell us that she was an alcoholic and was going to a meeting. That was not going to happen. I reflect back to this time with greater understanding and sorrow for my aunt, cousin, and uncle.

# SELF-SABOTAGE

My son was always worried about disappointing his father. He loved and idolized his father; yet there was one disappointment after another. It did not matter how much yelling and screaming happened; this became an ongoing saga when he was using.

My son was self-sabotaging. When he was using, he seemed to have a certain degree of insanity. His father was always the first person he stole from, which I could never understand. It was always a "WTF?" moment. It was almost as if he thought he did not deserve to hear anything less than his father's yelling. He continued to sabotage himself.

Disappointing his father was something my son did very often. The long, hard road was trying to get his father to understand that this was a disease. I never understood why my husband was so resistant about coming to that conclusion. I kept trying to convince him, to no avail. Please do not misunderstand; my husband always came through for my son, but there would be a lot of fighting first. That confused me, and I can only imagine how confusing it was for my son. My husband did a lot of saying one thing and then doing another. It was very, confusing.

My husband had many anger issues when it came to our son's disease. He was a nonbeliever for years. He believed our son could control his addiction. Many people feel that way, but I realized that my son was way beyond that. A lot of my friends say their fathers would not have put up with it either. I understand that, but my husband and I did not agree at all on how to handle our son. My husband truly did not know how to handle his frustration. The frustration level with this kind of situation is something for which no parent can prepare. People will tell you that you have to use tough love and eliminate the person from your life altogether. That is much easier said than done.

# DREAMS

Some unsympathetic people will chalk it off as my son's mistake, and say that it is a simple matter: he paid for his mistake. Yes, he did—to the tenth degree. My son had hopes and dreams. As his addiction progressed, his hopes and dreams became shadows that he could barely hold onto. People who knew us did not realize how dark the times for our family had become.

Someone said the definition of depression "is when someone can no longer see a future for himself." That line struck me hard and summed it all up. That is exactly where my son was mentally.

When I mentioned this to my psychiatrist, he moved his head back and forth, saying, "Well, that is not exactly what the definition of depression is."

No, that may not be how it is defined in the textbooks, but my son could no longer see a future for himself. It was as simple as that for him. He had gone too far over the edge, and he was definitely in the final stages of his disease.

# WALK THE WALK

They say that addicts have to want to get better and have to want to stop. It is true. They have to do it on their own, and they have to face reality, but that is way too painful when you have hit stage 4. Getting him into a program was not possible; remember what I said about insurance. People in recovery must be able to cope to get back on track in society. The addict's reality is legal crap, the bills that pile up, the people they steal from, how his friends view him, and a big lack of self-esteem. My son had clean friends and drug friends. Those two worlds were miles apart. How people accepted him was crucial for him. He would go into hiding, and his old friends did not know where he was or if he were still alive.

However, my son's music partner did visit often, expressing his concern. I would sit and listen and say nothing because there was nothing I could do. I knew he was not well. This friend did not turn his back on my son. He was always very disappointed when my son relapsed. The friend put together a collection of my son's writing and poetry and presented it to us at his funeral. The words he wrote in the prologue showed the hopes and dreams that eluded my son toward the end. His words were:

> He was incredibly talented. To me it was most evident when it came to watching him sing and write lyrics to songs we were working on. It seemed to just come through him, like he was channeling a deep connection to one's heart and soul. There were times he didn't have time to write down a thing at all, and he would just be in the moment and start singing, all the while weaving stories that really meant something and were truly remarkable. He brought light and joy to the

room, and when he performed it was captivating. I was
so fortunate to have been part of this process. He will
be missed the rest of my life.

Then he signed his name. I found it very touching that he took the
time to write this positive note at a time when we all felt such a loss for
words.

"Normal" people do not know what to do with addicts who return
to society. They are very skeptical. I understand the idea of clean friends
and family, but I advise everyone to understand that your friend is not
the person you remember. You have to dig down deep inside to find
the person you remember. He is in there; keep digging. That person
certainly would not have gotten himself into this kind of shit. The sad
story is that these clean friends, all of them, have said to me, "If I only
knew then what I know now, I would have done things differently."

My son had some great friends, lifelong friends, people who loved
him, family who adored him, and nobody knew what to do for him
when he relapsed. It is an unfortunate lesson that these friends have
learned since his death. He always knew that people were disappointed
in him when he relapsed, and it was a shame he could never rise above.
He became more and more ashamed of himself as time went on. Legally,
financially, socially, and spiritually, he was spent, gone, depleted.

Even though relapse is part of the disease, it becomes more and
more destructive each time.

# TREAD LIGHTLY

I learned early on that I had to think about the consequences of my words and actions. Yelling and screaming did not help, although I continued to express frustration. I thought very carefully about what I was going to say because I never wanted my son to run out of the house frightened and scared. It was obvious that he was already frightened, and God knows I was always scared out of my mind. I never knew what would come next.

Therefore, I used the kid-glove approach. Right or wrong, that is what I felt I had to do. There were people in my life that did not approve and certainly did not understand how I dealt with my son. He would be gone for days, and I would be terrified. It was for my own sanity that I did not push him away when he relapsed. Instead, I always tried to draw him closer. Once he left our sight, anything was possible. I was constantly frightened. Like others in similar situations, I did not know what to do. We had tried it all; we were just an inch short of having somebody sit with him all day and slap him around if he even looked like he needed to use. There are people who will do that. They are called "cleaners." They are very expensive. They are usually hired by high-profile people with a lot of money. It sounds nice, but that was not realistic.

# Rehab Centers

Please remember, that the rehab programs you see on TV are not available to the ordinary person.

I tried to follow the guidelines provided by all the rehabilitation programs. However, not every addict responds the same way. I tried everything from tough love to enabling to making him suffer the consequences and sending him to jail to tough love and enabling again to jail again and back to rehab. This went on for years, while I tried to keep a smile on my face and not let this take over my life.

It took a great toll on my relationships with my family. I was the "monkey in the middle" between my son and his father. My poor mother was destroyed to see her grandson struggle so much; it broke her heart. She would take to her sickbed.

At one point, I could not even talk to her. She could always sense in my voice when something was wrong. I hesitated to tell her what was going on, especially if it was bad news, and bad news was all I ever had. Given how much my son loved my mother and father, it seems unbelievable that he stole from them too, but indeed he did. I knew he loved his grandparents and me and his father and sister very much. All drugs have a long list of side effects and lying, stealing, and manipulating are side effects of this drug.

# THE CAT IS OUT OF THE BAG

When I was working back in the late 1990s, my son's addiction had become impossible for me to keep from my coworkers. I finally let the cat out of the bag and told them what was going on in my life. One of the younger staff members, who was only about four years older than my son, cried as I gave them the rundown. My coworkers were shocked. People like me did not have addicts in their families.

I was very fond of this young woman, who said to me, "How could he do this to you if he loves you so much?"

I said to her, "Honey, you know what? I know my son loves me, which is something that I have never questioned, but I'm telling you right now that if he was using and needed some dope, he would sell me on the street for a bag of dope."

That sounds horrible, but it was true. I was not delusional. Remember, at first you feel they are doing this to you. Then, as time goes on, you realize they are doing this to themselves.

Once I was in the office kitchen with one of my young coworkers. I looked over the table and said to her, "Mattie, someday I'm going to bury my son."

That statement just came out of the blue. Why I said it is a question I cannot answer. There would be many similar statements in my future. After my son died, Mattie called to wish me a Happy Mother's Day, and asked if I remembered saying that to her.

Yes, I did. I had a strong premonition about his fate from the beginning.

# Night and Day

When my son was clean, he would tell me how awful he felt about using his God-given charisma to do bad things. During those times, my husband and I always thought we would get our son back. We could see that kind soul again, and the difference between the two personalities was amazing. In the blink of an eye, we would forget everything bad that he had ever done to us. We would just bask in the sunlight of his handsome face and his clean, beautiful smile.

My son let everything spill out. When he was clean, it was as if he had taken truth serum, and he would tell me about the things he had done and seen. I never knew what to do about his confessions. After hearing his stories, I realized my son had almost died multiple times and did terrible things. His confessions and the things he discussed with me were gut-wrenching horrors. I kept them to myself for fear of getting him in trouble with his father.

Once my son told me that he'd been in a park downtown. He had just scored a bag of dope. He mentioned the vehicle he had at that time, so I know about when this took place. He looked around for some water to cook his dope. There was a puddle in the road, and he went to the puddle and took some water to cook his heroin. He shot up, and then did not wake up until the next day.

All I could think about was the lack of respect he had for himself, his safety, and his body. Addicts steal from themselves too. How could I feel so much sympathy for this young man who had no self-respect? It was puzzling.

I said to him, "Are you absolutely out of your mind? Do you realize that even after you cooked that stuff, you shot all that filth [from the puddle] into your veins?" How desperate does someone have to be to do that? That was one incident of many. He was really desperate when he needed dope.

Sometimes he and I would pass a drugstore or fast-food restaurant, and he'd pick cigarette butts out of the outdoor ashtrays. It made my skin crawl. The life he lived was beyond my comprehension. I'd ask what he was doing and tell him it was disgusting. Then I would buy him a pack of cigarettes.

His stealing and lying made people who loved him feel they could not trust him. When someone becomes an addict, all trust disappears. My son often was told in rehab that trust is not easy to get back, and I know he knew this.

When my son was clean, his dad was one of the hardest to win over. My husband could be very hard on him, sometimes too hard. Sometimes, though, I wonder if we played good cop/bad cop without realizing it. It became an automatic reaction; whenever my husband saw my son's eyes twinkling, he thought he was up to something, and of course that something had to be no good. It was a reflex response my husband could not seem to control.

# PLAY THE TAPE

When I started to write this book, my main objective was to research the people, places, and things that existed in my son's life. I soon realized that was ridiculous, since I'd lived the whole ordeal right along with him. I know my son was in situations I probably do not even want to imagine.

I will only discuss the things I know to be true. I have access to many of his old running partners. The last time around, there was quite a large group of them. Most were drug users who had been clean for a couple of years. None of them had struggled with addiction as long as my son had; they were novices in comparison. I could tell when I talked to them that my son left quite an impression on each one. He often talked about wanting to be clean and striving to be clean, but failing to be clean. I am sure some of them are clean today because he scared the shit out of them.

His friends were very kind and told me I could call them at any time and ask for information.

Many of them have been out of the life for a couple of years now, and I don't think it's fair to make them rehash the past. They were nice but misguided young people. My son often brought them to the house and introduced them without identifying them as addicts. He'd tell me afterward, "The poor guy has a drinking problem." One girl who could not muster up the strength to say much had a "brain tumor." At one point, he brought over a young woman who kept nodding off during dinner. "That was because she was in a car accident, and she had some brain damage."

That was the kind of shit he would tell me. I'd say to him, "Come on! I am not stupid." I always wondered why he thought an alcohol addiction or a brain tumor was so much better than drug addiction. Many times I'd see my son nod off. When I said to him, "You are nodding off," he would open his eyes wide and say, "No, I am not." I am not stupid. I know what nodding off looks like.

Many of them were nice young people with hopes and dreams; they became addicted and caught his disease. Thankfully, they were able to recover.

I occasionally go onto Facebook and look at their posts. These people are hardly recognizable. Twenty to thirty pounds makes a big difference in a person's appearance. In their posts, they continue to celebrate their sobriety. They will announce such things as "it has been two years since I've used."

If you are in recovery, you must play the tape of self-affirmation every day. Never stop celebrating your sobriety. That is not something that my son did. He believed, as time went on, that he could just forget it, but it does not happen that way. He always found it shameful to admit that he was a recovering addict. He would tell new friends that he'd had some demons in his past. He never mentioned what those demons were. I think he should have. That is why he needed to play the tape of self-affirmation. Former addicts need to remind themselves how nasty their lives used to be. You do not have to play the whole tape, only enough to remind yourself that you can never have just one. That is one lesson that rehab centers taught me: play the tape.

# THE WONDER YEARS

There was a time in my son's life when he remained drug-free for almost three years. He was living the life I had always wanted for him—a life he deserved, one filled with love, friends, fun, and dignity. He had self-respect and a job; best of all, he was the bright light we all remembered.

It was a wonderful time, and people asked me how I got him to stop. I would say, "I don't know; he just stopped." I always thought that I should say, "Shhh," I thought we would break a spell and jinx him if we discussed it too much. I was always waiting for the other shoe to drop. It is not a nice way to think about your child's recovery, but we had been through some pretty crappy stuff. Relapse is part of the disease. I became very realistic about addiction. It was something that had been shoved in my face very early on.

All I wanted was to bask in the light of my son's sobriety when he was sober. I just wanted to rejoice. We certainly did not need people to prophesy to our family. Many years ago, I used the phrase "can't cope, shoot some dope." That was how realistic I had to become. That is what the disease of addiction tells addicts to do.

# THE CLEAN AND THE DIRTY

My son was not able to maintain the mindset of a sociopath when he was clean. This is where the coping skills come into play. Unless you lived his life, my life, and my family's lives, you cannot understand. When my son was a child I made very sure that I taught him right from wrong as did all the other people in his life. We were not liars or thieves, or manipulative people. The fact that he became a heroin addict came from way out in left field.

Rehab counselors suggested we kick him out of the house, not answer the phone when he called from jail, etc. I was never good at tough love; it was not in my nature.

Since my son's death, people have said to me repeatedly, "Everything happens for a reason. Someday you will know the reason he lived his life the way he did, and why he died the way he did." They tell me that when I go to the "other side," wherever that other side is, I will learn the reason. In other words, I have to die before I can understand why this happened. Could there possibly be a good reason? I know I am not yet at that justification phase. I hope I will find that kind of peace.

Bottom line, I realize that my son lived the way he did and eventually reached stage 4 addiction. My son was honest with me when we were alone. He often expressed his pain, the loss of his dreams, and his loss of self-dignity.

When he was sober and struggling, I said to him, "You and I have heard wonderful stories of recovery and if anybody has the ability to recover, you do. You just have to get yourself to the point where you feel you are deserving of recovery."

The key phrase is "deserving of recovery." He got beyond that point. Meaning that he was deserving of recovery. When my son was clean, he gave us the sense that he had a lot of control and fortitude, and we believed that he could pull off just about anything. Staying clean seemed to be the one thing he could not conquer.

# CLEAN FRIENDS, DIRTY FRIENDS

When my son was clean, he had many, many friends. When he relapsed, he would go into hiding. Shame made him go underground. It was as if he disappeared off the face of the earth. He went deep into the drug culture, another place, with a whole other group of people—people like him, unfortunately, who were lost. If we think about it and have any compassion at all, that is sad.

Those who go out and get ripped on a Saturday night do not realize they are putting themselves at risk; many people do not realize that alcoholism is also a mess of an addiction. My psychiatrist refers to alcohol as the "dirty drug." That Jekyll and Hyde thing you see in people who drink too much—I have been there and done that.

Alcohol can be as lethal as any other drug, but people look at drinking differently. Obtaining a bottle of booze is not on the same level as seeking a drug. There are liquor stores on every corner. The bottom line is that your drug of choice—whatever it is—can completely ruin your life.

Young people do not understand how easily they can become hooked on these poisons and how vulnerable they are. I stand firm in my conviction that nobody takes that first drink or snort, smokes that first cigarette, plays that first slot machine, or watches that first porn with the intention of becoming an addict. It is just not that much fun. It can become a very dark world.

# THE ENABLER

People often use the word *enabler* when discussing addiction. I probably am considered the grand enabler. God knows, the word is used all the time in rehab, and I have spent a lot of time thinking about it. What is an enabler? Who is the enabler? What does it mean? Why do people enable?

Webster's definition of *enable* is to make able; to give power, means, or ability; to make competent; to make possible or easy; to empower a person to do what he or she would otherwise be incapable of doing.

In my son's case, I was helping him do what he would otherwise be incapable of doing—recover. Enabling was everything I was trying to do. I wanted to give him the will to overcome his disease. I wanted to keep him alive. None of the people in rehab ever saw his behind-the-scenes activities. He did not need an enabler to get his drugs. He did that all on his own, with no assistance, and he had that down to a science. He needed mental-health care.

What is the difference between unconditional love and enabling? In my mind, there is a very fine line between the two because no matter how many times he fell, no matter how many times he stole from me or lied to me, I still loved him unconditionally. I never forgot the truly awesome human being he could have been but unfortunately had forgotten. It was my son who could not love himself unconditionally.

The definition of the word *unconditional,* in the dictionary is very simple: not limited by conditions, absolute, complete, innate, and natural, and the conditioning of the individual.

It will always bother me that, as his mother, I could not convince him he had a reason to live. Yelling and screaming only drove him deeper into addiction; a lot of shouting went on at different times in our home. At the end of his life, my son suffered from a debilitating mental illness, particularly depression, and he may have been bipolar. As I said earlier, because he had no insurance, he had no options.

I still do not understand why some people have such burdens tossed at them while others sail through life without any hardship. Do we really make our own beds and then lie in them? That question will remain unanswered for me until the day I die. I want people to understand that my son was a normal young man, not an actor or a rock star. This book could be about your child.

# TOUGH LOVE

As my son's addiction continued, I struggled each day to keep it together, to keep myself grounded, so that I would be there to pick him up when he started to slip and slide. I guess some might call that a type of enabling, but trying to keep someone alive is not enabling that person. I walked around with a net under my son for sixteen years. I did not know what else to do; it just became second nature to me. They throw that "tough love" terminology around, but they never define it or reveal how tough you have to be.

When my son went to jail for the first time, I was devastated. A person who headed one of the programs told me if he called, I should not accept the charges.

The next morning was a Saturday. I got the phone call from the operator, who said, "You are receiving a collect call from an inmate at the jail. Do you accept the charges?"

I did not realize that my son was listening, waiting to hear whether I would accept those charges. I said no, and then I heard him on the line. I hung up. It was one of the worst days of my life. I cried all day.

There should be resources for people like my son. When someone continues to exhibit negative behavior, and suffers the consequences of that behavior, it should be obvious that he has some type of mental illness. There should be a law to mandate help for people with mental-health issues, whether or not they have health insurance. What kind of insight do you need before you determine that a person might have mental-health issues after ten years of heroin abuse? If a person is admitted to the same emergency room three times in one year, the medical professionals who tend to that person should question whether he is trying to kill himself. Should not that warrant a mental-health exam? I think it should.

# I KNEW

I often let my son borrow my car and drive me to work. It always seemed safer for me to let him borrow my car than for him to take the bus or walk to the city to score a bag of dope. I never knew what kind of trouble he might get into if he were on foot. I figured there would be some accountability if he had my car. He had to pick me up from work at a certain time and, at least from that point on, I would have my hands on him.

One morning, not long before he died, I was driving to work, and he was sitting in the passenger seat. My keys hang very low. As the keys touched my leg, they would rattle because I was shaking so much.

My son said to me, "Mom, do I make you do that?"

I looked at him and said, "Yes, I guess you do. I shake all the time."

Another time I picked him up at his apartment. I had to take a major highway I did not know well, and I really disliked that route. We had almost gotten to my workplace, and I turned down a side road, in what I would describe as a rough neighborhood. As I was driving down the street, my son slid down onto the car floor faster than if he had been shot.

I looked at him and said, "'What the hell?" I knew why he did that. He had seen one of his drug dealers on the street. He probably owed the dealer a bundle. I had been told, more than once, that he would wear out his welcome with the dealers. He was just as manipulative with them as he was with anyone else. It is not easy to be the mother of a heroin addict. It would have been a lot easier if I had not loved him so much. I loved him more than life itself. He was my son.

# DESTINY

Sometimes I think my son was destined to live this life; it was fated in a way. It seemed like a Greek tragedy. "Legends that teach the futility of trying to outmaneuver an inexplicable fate that has been correctly predicted." I do not remember where I got that sentence from, but when I read it, it just felt like it fit him. I knew that was my son. That is a painful thing for me to say about my own son, but it became my truth and reality.

I thought I had pretty much gone through it all. I have nearly gone "over the edge" many times, but my son's death caused more grief than I ever imagined. He was thirty-four when he died. Few people knew his battle as well as I did. I paid very close attention. No matter what, you cannot imagine the pain when your child succumbs to death.

In a lot of ways, my son and I had very similar temperaments, so I had a clear picture of what would ensue. There was so much frustration seeing him hurt himself repeatedly. I used to say to him all the time, "Why do you keep doing this to yourself over and over again?"

Our family has been through hell and back a couple of times, and they were painful, major, life-changing events. Some of these events caused terrible alienation between my family members.

# FAMILY

Family members often seem to blame the parents of the addict. Many people cannot accept the fact that addiction is a disease. They feel that an addict chooses to misbehave, act out, and be self-indulgent. The truth is that an addict's life sucks. Why anyone would choose to live this way is a mind-bender. Do not get me wrong; I realize it is an addict's decision to try the drug that first and second time. That is why I was confused about my son, who seemed to be a level headed young man. There is guilt involved, and there is great pain involved—physical, mental, and financial. The lack of funds becomes a big burden. There is anger; there is fear; and there is plain, good, old-fashioned family dysfunction.

Some of my stories will probably cause more friction between my family members. When my son was clean, he was with his sister all the time, but when he was dirty, she would not even speak his name. My belief is that when you love someone, especially a child, you love him or her good, bad, or indifferent. The phrase "I'd jump in front of a train for my child" represents exactly how I felt. Throughout my life, I have loved many people unconditionally; perhaps that was unhealthy. But I was raised that way; at least I thought I was.

My parents loved my son immensely. That was always very evident; he was their baby, and he was the firstborn grandson. The relationship he had with my parents was one any child would hope for, and he loved them very much. It truly was not because of a lack of love that my son fell short of what he could be. No one thing triggered his addiction. No one who saw pictures of him would ever believe that he'd become a heroin addict. He certainly would not have been picked out of a lineup. I really thought the sensitivity he had as a child would work for him as he grew up and into adulthood. In a positive way, I believed he would always be a good boyfriend, a decent friend, and a decent son, but that was not the case.

Was he too sensitive? Was he not tough enough? This is where my guilt comes in. I always felt responsible for giving him the confidence and the constitution to get through life. Once he became a full-blown addict, he could not handle the things that life threw at him, so he resorted to self-medication. This is the issue that haunts me—the self-anesthetizing. Many people come home from a bad day at work, sit down, and say, "God, I've got to have a drink, Good Lord, what a miserable day at work." If you do your cleaning on a Saturday and you are a cigarette smoker, you take a break. You think, *I owe myself a cigarette.* It becomes a reward. Is that a bad habit or an addiction?

Food, drugs, sex, cigarettes, booze—they are all the same. They all become a reward or a pacifier for whatever life throws at us. I checked Webster's dictionary for the definition of addict, and found this: "Addict: to devote or give oneself, habitually or compulsively; to cause to become compulsively and physiologically dependent on a habit-forming substance; one who is addicted, as to narcotics, or a devoted believer or follower."

Next, I looked for the definition of addiction: "Addiction: The quality or condition of being addicted, especially to a habit-forming substance."

Just weeks before he died, my son and I had a text-messaging session, back and forth. I kept telling him that he deserved to be happy and asked why he thought he wasn't entitled to live a happy life.

He texted back, "Thanks, Mom, if it wasn't for you, I don't know how I could go on." Then he added, because he could sense my thought process: "I would never kill myself because I know it would kill you." Well, he broke his promise, but mentally he was severely compromised. I realize that now.

I knew he was not happy, and we were approaching the holidays. That was never a good time for him. He never did well at the holidays, and there was always some kind of crisis around that time of year. Everything changed dramatically after the death of my parents and, although he never spoke about it, their deaths affected him greatly. He got to the point where he felt he had nothing to live for—no way out financially or legally—and he had a girlfriend who was as much a mess as he was. It is hard enough taking care of one addict, let alone two, and that is the position he was in at that point. How can one drug addict trying to overcome his addiction take care of another addict? It is not possible.

# FOREVER

It was December 30, 2012, almost a year since my son died. I realized that I would never be the person I was when he was alive. Despite the fact that he made our lives very hectic for most of the sixteen years of his addiction, there is a big void in my life now that I've lost him to this disease. Yes, I had an innate sense that this was a chronic disease that would lead to his death. Still I was not prepared, how could I be?

Addiction has the power to destroy all that is good in a person's life.

# MOM AND DAD

My parents were two of the most important people in my son's life. He actually wrote, "And all fingers point to me" (see the chapter titled "Jail 2009"). I need to explain what he meant.

I always believed my mother and I were very close and that she loved me unconditionally. My mother had given birth to me when my father went into the army and was posted overseas. He got one brief look at me before he went away. There was no bonding time. He was young too. My mother and I lived with my grandparents. I remember that period of my lifetime with great fondness. No one ever made me feel as though I was an intrusion. I felt very much loved. I was a normal kid who moved out to the suburbs with her parents, went to parochial school, and learned my catechism like a good little Catholic school girl. I had my share of friends in school, and I thought my childhood was wonderful.

My mother adored me, and I knew nothing would ever change that. I had a great childhood. I grew up in an awesome little area off the bay. I have fond memories. I remember walking down to the park with my parents to watch the fireworks on July 4.

My father did not have much to do with my upbringing. He was usually working. He was a radio announcer, and that got me in good with the nuns at school. They listened to his shows in the morning. They all got such a big kick out of him.

My poor mom suffered many miscarriages before she gave birth to my sister ten years later. I was delighted when she was born; finally, I had a sister. But by the time she was born, my mother was ten years older than she'd been when she had me. In a way, we were raised by two different sets of parents.

My mother wore the pants in the family. She sometimes had a raging Irish temper. Life went on. My sister grew up. My father got a new job, which transferred him to a new area. He seemed to be making more money, but the move never sat well with my mother. We had quite a family network where we lived, and leaving was not something that she took kindly to at all.

In fact, my father commuted back and forth three to four hours on weekends for more than two years before we even considered moving. I was sixteen, and they practically had to throw me in the trunk to get me to move. Sixteen is not a good time to move. I was a junior in high school, with only a year and a half to go.

# SIBLING

Because of our age difference, my sister and I were subject to two different sets of rules. My parents were mellower by the time my sister came along. I do not remember ever resenting that fact. I turned out to be the mealy-mouthed one, who was yelled at more for rolling my eyes than for actually saying anything. My sister was much more verbal. She would tell you what she thought. Again, I had no ill feelings about this. I was who I was, and she was who she was. At least she was honest about her feelings. I always gave her credit for saying what she felt.

What does this have to do with my son? I bring up my childhood to set the stage for what happened after my mother died. My mother was diagnosed with lung cancer in 2002. This was not a big surprise, although it was heartbreaking.

She was a cigarette smoker, two packs a day. That was my mom's addiction. To be honest, I vacillate between giving up cigarettes and picking them up again myself. My mother's illness was not only a tragedy for me but also for my family; my son was devastated. This was a very terrible time in our lives because the thought of losing my mother seemed truly overwhelming. She was in and out of the hospital numerous times with all sorts of problems and complications. My son was still using when my mother was diagnosed.

Early one morning, my husband and I got a disturbing phone call from my father, who said that our son had broken into the house and stolen money from them. My mother was in the hospital. My son was upstairs in his room. He was not aware of the phone call. I asked myself how I would handle this. I had never planned on keeping this a secret. I always approached my son very carefully when this kind of situation happened. I had to have my hands on him if I wanted to get any answers. There was no doubt in my mind that my son took the money; that was not even a question. I was standing in our kitchen with my daughter, who was going off to high school; my husband was in the shower. All of a sudden, someone came through the downstairs door, yelling and screaming. It was my sister. My father had called my sister and told her what happened. She came into our house like a demon from hell.

My sister came barreling up the stairs, yelling, "Where is_____?" She opened the door to his stairwell and said, "You get down here right now!"

He came to the bottom of the stairs, and she started to hit him and scream at him. My poor daughter was going crazy, completely unglued and wondering what was happening, and my husband was still in the shower. My sister was screaming and hitting my son, who rolled up into a ball in the stairwell.

My sister kept yelling, "You ruined my Christmas!"

Talk about confusing. What the hell, did that have to do with anything? He ruined most of our Christmases. If he was not in the ER, he was in jail.

I got my husband out of the shower, and he told my sister that if she did not leave the house, he would call the police. By the time she left, my son had run upstairs. He jumped out a second-story window and took off. I do not remember how long he was gone. I have no idea if I would have called the police. I went out looking for my son and I did not know where the hell he was. I knew he was probably using to kill the pain of the horrible thing he had done. Stealing from his grandparents seemed so desperate.

You may ask how I maintained sanity. I had no choice. Someone had to keep her shit together. I had become good at acting like I was okay when I truly was not; that is an acquired talent.

After work, I went to the hospital to visit my mother. She looked up at me and said, "I heard the story about your son." I had not intended to mention it because I did not want to upset her. I knew how much she loved him. My father and sister told her the story. Now, what my son did was more than awful, but remember that there are two sides to a story.

Calm and controlled, my mother and I discussed the situation. I explained that while what my son did was more than horrible, my sister's behavior was also ridiculous and caused more harm than good. Her handling of the situation was very wrong. I did not expect anybody to keep the theft a secret, but her behavior was really over the top. As far as I was concerned, my son was certainly wrong, but so was my sister. My mother did not agree. I felt that we had to agree to disagree.

After this incident, my son was on a "full run," as I liked to call it. Mom did not call me, and I did not call her. I felt terrible about this, but my mother did not see the type of chaos that my sister brought into our house that morning. That was when I realized my sister was the keeper of my parents money.

My husband went to my parents' home during a snowstorm and plowed their driveway in order to break the ice. I called my mother after that; I could not let this go on. She was my mother, and I loved her. We eventually rekindled our relationship, but it was never the same. It was obvious that my parents' health was starting to fail. Mom had lung cancer, and Dad had multiple strokes.

I always had the impression that my parents were angrier with us than they were with our son. When my mother and I talked about my son's addiction, she would always say, "I don't know how you do it." I was more than confused, but I knew she was not the same person she had been before her cancer surgery. Thankfully, she lived another four years after that point.

****

My son got clean in 2005. When my mother died, he was clean. I was always very grateful for that. It meant a lot to my mother, and it meant a lot to me. My beautiful mother died in June 2006. She died in a hospital bed that we put in the living room of my parents' home. I was with her the night before.

I remember the morning she died as if it were yesterday. I could tell it was time, and I called everybody in the family—my son at work, my daughter and husband, my sister and her husband and children—and told them to come to the house quickly. We were all there, except for my dad, who was recovering from a broken hip. We had lost the matriarch of our family, and that was more than painful. I did not know what I was going to do without her, but I knew I had to go on.

My husband, our son and daughter, and I went to the hospital to tell my father. That was not easy. I was worried about my son. This was his grandmother, and he loved her. Losing her was a big deal for him. He loved my mother and father so much, and I did not know how he was going to react, but I think he felt he needed to stay strong for me. I wish he hadn't.

We made the funeral arrangements and took my father out of the hospital. After my mom died, I was devastated. I felt that I needed to go into my parents' house and mourn alone. I deserved to do that. I had known my mother since she was eighteen years old.

I had lost my mom and wanted to walk around the house that she would never walk around again. I had a special relationship with my mom. I had trouble believing she had actually died. I went up to my mother's room and looked at all the pictures of her and the kids that she had on the desk. The canvas bag she carried back and forth to work was lying on the floor. In the bottom of the bag was a letter. My natural impulse was to read it, so I did. My mother had beautiful handwriting; as soon as I saw it, I knew it was hers.

This was not a letter; it was a rough draft of my mother's will. I realized after reading it that my mother must have been very angry with me. I was dumbfounded. I always thought that my sister and I would split everything equally after our parents passed. It never crossed my mind that we would not. I never questioned it. It was not that my parents had a lot of money, and it was not the money that upset me. It was the tone of her words. It was clearly the tone of a woman who was very angry with her daughter, and I didn't even know it.

Naturally, I was upset and called my sister. I said, "Oh my God, I found this letter that Mom wrote, and she sounds really upset with me."

My sister asked what I was doing snooping around the house. I thought, *What? You have to be kidding me.*

Another night I was at the house talking to my father; my sister called, and I picked up the phone. She and I got into it, and she said, "Just leave the key there." I had to leave the key to my parents' home, and my sister would not allow me to return. Again, I did not speak up.

One Sunday I stopped by the house to talk to my father. Afterward, my father told my sister I wanted him to change his will. That was not true. That doesn't even sound like me, as anyone who knows me knows. My father was devastated by my mother's death, and he really did not have all of his mental faculties.

One day my father said to me, "Well, your sister was close to your mother. She and your mother went to the store and out together all the time."

When my son was young, my mom and I were together constantly. No my father would not remember that because he was never around.

I said to my father, "Well, she can do that. She doesn't work."

My father replied, "Well, maybe you shouldn't have."

Right then and there I knew where the conservation was going. I worked so it was my fault that my son was an addict. Now you may think I was paranoid, but I was correct. I was fighting a losing battle.

Earlier I'd told my sister that my husband and I had thought about this, and maybe Dad shouldn't be alone. "He can move in with us."

My sister said, "No, Mom wanted him to stay in the house."

"Okay," I said.

To make this long story shorter, my sister and her husband made me take them to court to get the $50,000 that my mother and father left for me. My mother died in 2006, and my dad died in 2007. My son was clean, but I was very surprised at the way he grieved when his grandparents died. I would have expected him to throw himself over my mother's casket at her funeral, but he was very stoic. I never asked my son for any allegiance after all that transpired with my family. I never even discussed it with him because I did not want him to feel responsible for what had happened, but he knew, and I think this hurt him very deeply. Talk about guilt. I believe that is why he wrote, "All fingers point to me." I do not blame anyone but my son for his relapse or death. That was on him. I am just describing his mindset at that time. It was truly a difficult time for everyone.

# FALLING OUT

Through the years of my son's addiction, he made many trips to the emergency room, probably too many to mention. I am sure there were many ER trips I do not know about. I found out about one by mistake after he died. It stands out in my mind, and I think you will understand why. In 2011, an ambulance took him to the emergency room after a heroin overdose. This is part of the report from one of the emergency room doctors:

> This patient was signed out to me by my co-resident. This is a thirty-three-year-old male, status post-heroin overdose, was found by EMS in a car, after they received a call and brought in by the EMS [emergency medical services]. He has been here in the emergency department over nine hours. Overnight, the patient sobered up clinically from whatever substance he was intoxicated or under the influence of. However, a safety sit was initiated and all visitors banned for this patient because his girlfriend was found to have given him an unknown substance in our ED [emergency department], which made him more drowsy, while they were in the A12 bed. Doctor did find an empty syringe in his room lying next to him. The girlfriend was suspected to have given him some substance that made him drowsier. She was escorted out, and a safety sit initiated.

As far as I am concerned, there is something wrong with this report. I hope that ERs have changed their protocols since that time. I'm sure there were many times when my son woke up after having consumed

74

pills, alcohol, and probably a number of bags of heroin, and said to himself, *What the fuck; how am I still here?*

It seemed ironic that after all the years he had been using that he did not die from a drug overdose. I had often thought that some night I would get that dreaded phone call telling me that someone found him dead in a back alley somewhere. My son did not wind up being one of those stories. All I ever wanted was for him to stop. I realize now that I had no control; only my son had the control. Looking back, I realize he did not have that potential, not without the mental help he needed.

# HAMSTER WHEEL

One truth I know is the more you use, the more you lose, and the more you lose, the more you use. It is what I call the hamster wheel. It just keeps going around and around and around, and then it spins so fast the addict can't jump off or does not want to.

God knows how many times I thought that if I took just one drug, every horrible feeling and mistake in my life would go away. I would not feel physical or emotional pain, and I would not have to think about it. That is what happens to addicts. They create so much havoc and turmoil in their lives that they do not want to get off the hamster wheel. Sobriety becomes painful. The problem is that in the process of killing the pain, they kill their souls. You have to be a good sociopath to be a good addict, and a good addict to be a sociopath. I do not believe that my son was either. I truly believe he had a conscience. If he'd had less of a conscience, he might be alive today.

# THE CRITICS

At one point, we had some very narrow-minded neighbors who believed my husband and I were responsible for our son's addiction. They thought we were bad parents, and that was why he was an addict.

It is important to understand that my husband and I did not just let this happen. When this kind of crisis takes place in your home, you do not have the slightest clue about what is best or worst for your child. Anyone who thinks my son continued on his path because of a lack of love and concern is truly mistaken. Addiction hurts the whole family—mother, father, sister, aunts, uncles, and grandparents. Nobody ever agrees on what steps to take. We tried them all.

People should not speak about situations they know nothing about. As a human being and as his mother, this was the most defining thing that ever happened in my life.

# CHOICE

I use the word *choice* very carefully when referring to an addict. That experimental stage is definitely a choice, but nobody takes that first drink, hydrocodone pill, vial of crack, or bag of heroin with the idea of becoming an addict. It is a tortured way to live.

He was gentle, considerate, and loving, but his heroin addiction took him to the depths of hell.

# COURT

To explain just how bad the legal situation got, I will describe our experience in court. We would sit in a room filled with people. There was usually a clerk standing next to the judge. She was responsible for handing the folder for the next case to the judge. I knew every time my son was about to be called to the bench because he had the thickest folder. I would nudge him and say, "You're next," when I saw the clerk pull the folder. Now I might sound a little flippant about this, and please realize this is not my intention, but I became immune. It had become such a major part of my life. Strength was something I cultivated over time. It was not something I was born with. I was the only person who realized his decline. I became the great pretender.

I did not let on until it got so bad there was no denying it. I tried to keep my faith. At that point, it had to be up to God. In my son's mind, there was no reason for him to stay clean.

Once in October 2011 I went outside with a coworker to smoke a cigarette. I blurted out, "I think my son is losing his battle with addiction." She said nothing. She knew about his addiction, and she probably knew that statement came from my gut. You might say, if I knew so much about the disease and about the person with the disease, why didn't I do something? You name it, I had done it.

# THE SANCTITY OF JAIL

In the early years of my son's disease, I did anything I could to keep him out of jail. I thought that jail was the worst thing in the world for him. It frightened the crap out of me. As his disease progressed and the years went, I was relieved when he went to jail. At least I knew where he was and that he would be clean for forty-five days. He'd get out of jail about fifteen pounds heavier, bright-eyed, and clear headed, which always gave him (and me) hope that things would change. He always started off with the best intentions. He'd attend meetings and go to outpatient programs, but something always seemed to pull him back.

Why did he feel the continued need to self-medicate? Somebody makes the mistake of trying a drug, and before he knows it, he is a full-blown addict. It has taken over his whole being, lifestyle, and world. It becomes his mother, father, and lover. It becomes all consuming.

# HIGH ALERT

Even when my son was clean, I was always on alert. I was always in crisis mode. For years, that was all I knew. I had forgotten how to relax.

It was partially my own fault. Many times, we went to see him on family weekends at whatever program he was in, and several of his housemates had no visitors. I always felt bad, and my son would say, "The kid's parents don't talk to him anymore." The families cut their addicts off, and that is what the counselors told us to do.

But when he was in one of those programs, he was clean and just how we remembered him. One of my biggest shortcomings is that I forgive and forget too easily. After some clean time, he would convince me, and himself, that he would return to his normal self. He really meant it, and I really believed him.

# SHOCK

My son went to rehab after rehab, court-mandated treatments lasting ten months, and all sorts of outpatient programs. At one point in 2003, we found out that he had run up one of our credit cards. We had to press charges. He had to turn himself in. I arranged to take him to an officer who knew him.

I investigate options for him. I'd read an article in the paper about shock programs, which were run by the state's correctional facilities. These were non-gated correctional environments. Most of the young men there were drug offenders, either buyers and/or dealers. Most, if not all, had exhausted all other types of addiction facilities and programs. They were nonviolent felons, but they were all in trouble with the law. I thought my son needed something other than jail.

When I asked the police officer if my son qualified, he turned to another officer and asked if my son could qualify for a shock program.

The other police officer said, "Yeah, I don't see why not. He's a nonviolent felon."

*Thank God*, I thought. *At least, he is a nonviolent felon.* I was grateful that I could say that, which is sad. The police officer said he would take my son before the judge. I appreciated that because it meant we did not have to wait in the courtroom filled with people. They took him over to the jail but had to pull him out one day to make an appearance in another county. The judge in the other county ordered him into a shock program. Naturally, I went to that court appearance. I wanted to make sure I knew what was happening. There were a number of different facilities throughout the state. They held him in a prison until they decided which facility to assign him to.

Naturally, he was clean in the shock program. There were no bars. Most of the young men in the program were there due to drug crimes. When they got there, the authorities took one of their socks and put it in a paper bag; if someone tried to escape from the facility, they would have a dog sniff the sock and track the boy down. All of the boys were struggling for their lives, and this probably seemed like a last resort for them. I am sure some of them made it to recovery. Believe it or not, my son became his group's platoon leader. He was a leader. He always did well when he was clean; he seemed to thrive in a structured environment. Every other weekend, all three of us—my husband, the young woman I mentioned, and me—drove three-plus hours to see him.

The shock-treatment program had a graduation ceremony. He was released from that program in October 2004. I so hoped that his life of addiction was finished. He came home to us, and bam—reality hit. Now what? Now he was a convicted felon, and that is not a good situation to be in when you are looking for a job. Most job applications include the question, "Are you a convicted felon?

# JOB

My son got a job at a moving company. It certainly seemed benign enough. Now he was on probation. I kept my fingers crossed. Who knew that hydrocodone was a big problem in the moving business? I never even thought about it. Everyone had back pain. There was always a supply of pills in the moving truck. My son was right smack in the middle of where he had been. He started to use hydrocodone. I do not think people realize how closely linked hydrocodone is to heroin addiction. With any narcotic you run the risk of addiction, I do not care who you are. Now with heroin becoming so cheap we have a bigger problem.

Years ago when I worked at a physician's office, we had a list of patients who were called, "drug seekers." We kept that list by our phones, so that when they called for narcotics we could check to see how often they were prescribed. If they consumed too much, they would not get any more. I must admit, however, that we never did anything to help them, which is sad. I realize that now when I read ER reports. They sober them up, and then send them out the door. EMTs even give them Narcan at the scene to revive them, and off the addicts go.

# PAROLE

I was shocked to realize my son was now on parole, not probation. I had become accustomed to probation. Now we were in the big times. That was another indication of how bad his crimes were. Now he was a convicted felon. I had always thought that parole was for very bad criminals. What I did not realize was that he was a very bad criminal. I used to ask myself how he got like that. I am sure he asked himself the same question. That is not a nice thing for a parent to admit about her child. I certainly did not regard him as a criminal, unless he was using. But he was.

He had a no-nonsense parole officer. I will never forget him. He was my hero. He could do things I was not able to do. He would "call my son on his shit," as they say in the rehab world. He obviously had a lot of experience.

One night, I was alone in the house with my son. He did not go to a meeting, a planned drug testing, or whatever. Plus, when you are using you can just put these important issues aside. That is one of this drug's benefits—you don't care about anything. My son always had some lame excuse for not going to a meeting, and his parole officer would show up at the door. The parole officer was very kind to me but very stern. I had the feeling he knew my exact emotions over all of this and that I had a great amount of fear and anxiety. He would take over, and it was a great relief.

I always felt trapped and did not know how to get out of the mess. I certainly could not do this this recovery for him. If I could have, it would have been a done deal years ago. The parole officer asked, "Where is he?" I said he was upstairs. The parole officer walked up the stairs. I could hear him talking to my son. He tried to give him a drug test. My son had all sorts of excuses for not being able to pee; he always did.

Finally, the parole officer came down and said, "Mrs. Marks, would you please come upstairs with me for a second." I followed him into my son's room. There on the bed sat my son in handcuffs. His parole officer said to him, "Look at your mother," because at this point I was crying. My son was also crying; he had a look in his eyes that said, "Yep, I've done it again."

I have to admit I was relieved when the parole officer took him back to jail. It was a respite for me.

My son spent forty-five days in a jail he had never been in before. His parole officer insisted he go to a halfway house. Believe me when I say this halfway house was in drug heaven, and my son was with a group of people just like him. Although I was nervous because of the location, he finally started to walk the walk instead of just talk the talk.

# CLEAN TIME

While my son was in the halfway house, he got a job. He and his girlfriend of five years split. That was the young woman to whom I had become close. There was just too much water under the bridge. She was done, but she remained his friend until the end.

He was heading in the right direction. He did well at his job and made many new friends. You could tell he felt good about himself, and he was happy. He became fastidious about his job.

Rule of thumb is that you should get a plant after rehab. To make sure you can keep it alive before having a girlfriend

He met a young woman one night, and they fell madly in love. They became an item, as one may say. A short time after they met, they got a little apartment close to where he worked. I kept my mouth shut. He should have kept celebrating his sobriety and going to meetings. Please, this is most important.

They lived together for quite some time. She was a little younger than he was, but she was a great girl and was spunky and beautiful. They did all the things that I always wanted him to do. They went dancing; they did karaoke. They both had great voices, and they just had fun. He met her parents; she came to our house. Things seemed very normal for a while.

I have a picture of my son from Christmas 2005. He looked so happy. He looked so well. He looked better than he had in a long time and was even about twenty pounds heavier. The smile on his face was awesome. He got close to her family, and she did to ours. I was happy as long as he was.

He was fastidious about their apartment—cooking, cleaning, decorating, very proud to have a place of his own and to be living with her. The two of them were a lot of fun and seemed to be very good together. They had tons of friends; they would have Super Bowl parties in their tiny apartment, and the place would be packed with people. Everybody loved him. Everybody loved her too.

They often invited my husband and me over to dinner, which was such a pleasure. He was a great cook, and he got a lot of joy from inviting us to his place. It gave him a great sense of satisfaction. We never discussed much about the past or his behavior. I just presumed that he had told her about his "demons," as he referred to them. I do not know if she knew exactly how bad it had been in the past.

Naturally, all of his friends knew him as clean, awesome, and fun. Yes, he told some of them that he had demons in his past, but I do not think he ever went into detail. There were only a few old friends who knew his problem was heroin. He rekindled his old friendships, and everyone thought that was that. Simple! He just got over it. Wrong!

I wonder what those people thought his demon was. They saw him drink. They knew he smoked. One of his friends gave him hydrocodone for wisdom-tooth pain. I found that out after he died. None of them had any idea what addiction was about.

They all went out frequently as a group and celebrated their youth, and a lot of them drank too much. I realized he was drinking and smoking cigarettes. I always hoped the booze would not be an issue for him. I guess I looked at it as the lesser of the evils when it came to his addiction. There is that stupid misconception about booze again, but I knew it was not his drug of choice. He should not have been drinking. He kept in touch with us all the time, even though he was busy.

He was such a "take charge" person when he was clean. I do not think any of his friends knew or realized the significant change that could take place if he relapsed. They had no clue.

These clean years were his glory days. God, those were great years, and I look on back on them with great love and affection. This young woman will always remain in my heart as a person my son loved very much.

# STAGE 4

What happened? I will give you the series of events, as I know them. My son planned to ask his girlfriend to marry him. A close friend told him "she was a good time and a great girl but not the marrying type." Then my son, his girlfriend, and a friend went away; my son was having wisdom-tooth pain, and his friend gave him hydrocodone.

I bet my son thought he could handle it. After all, he was only taking them for pain. Wrong! Then my son had all four wisdom teeth removed, and the dentist gave him a prescription for hydrocodone. He should have refused them. Well needless to say that was that.

Somewhere along the line, his job became frustrating. That was the frosting on the cake. He took the business more seriously than he should have. No two ways about it, my son had a tendency to be a little OCD, but his boss was not. He was no longer a team player. He had too many complaints about the way things "were being done." My son had made a lot of friends there, but they all turned their backs on him.

He stopped working there and collected unemployment. He applied for other jobs, but word was out that he was blackballed. I will never know exactly what happened, but my son was arrested for stealing and sexual harassment. Stealing was possible, but sexual harassment, I do not believe. There was a lot of discussion on how they were going to "fix his wagon," so to speak. That was that, and he went into a full relapse.

His girlfriend asked, "When was the last time you spoke to your parents?" She knew it was not a good sign when he was distant from us. He also spent time away from her, which must have seemed very sketchy, considering that they always seemed to be joined at the hip.

He was doing that hiding thing that he often did when he relapsed. One day they came over. I made it very clear to him that I knew things were not well, and that there was a chance he was relapsing. She was standing right next to him.

I looked at him and said, "What are you going to do when you lose her?"

His response was, "I don't know, Mom." Well, he would soon find out.

He went into a full relapse, and she left him sometime in January 2009. The apartment went to shit, and he did not pay his bills. He owed his landlord a ton of money, and he needed to move out of the apartment. When my son was sober, he had developed a nice relationship with his landlord. He took good care of the grounds. I paid the $2,000 my son owed to his landlord, and he moved out.

# MOVING DAY

He took his time moving, and it made me very nervous. I knew it was a painful thing for him to move out of that apartment. Of course, he did not concentrate as much on moving as he did on scoring dope. That became his priority. He had to kill the pain he felt when he lost everything he had gained.

This drug becomes your lover, friend, mother, and every other significant person who was ever in your life. This drug becomes the substitute for anyone who may have been important to you. The pain of losing those people was gone when he used his drugs. His girlfriend was very mad at him. She certainly did not know what an addict's life could be like. How could she? She had lived with a sensible young man who was a provider and an upstanding citizen. Who could understand how something like that could happen to someone like him?

At one point in time, I worked with a young woman. It was about the time that I told my coworkers about my son. She and I were alone one day, and she asked, "Have you ever tried heroin?" Now I had done some experimenting, but that is something that was never presented to me. No, I answered. She told me that when she was a young girl she had been a heroin addict. She said that it was one of those drugs that, if the world were coming down on your head, you would not care. Was I shocked at her confession to me? I guess I was. Now I realize that she was trying to let me know that this was going to be a ballbuster.

He took too long moving out. He was obviously dragging his heels. That was an end of an era of the ending of very good times for him. One day, while his truck was backed up to the apartment door, two policemen walked into his apartment and picked him up on a bench warrant because he had not appeared in court. He was standing in the kitchen, near the door, which was open, and the jig was up. He never gave the police a hard time; he was always respectful and compliant in his dealings with them. They were not the enemy; heroin was.

When the officers patted him down, they found a switchblade. Lo and behold, not only was he taken in on the bench warrant, now they also had him on a weapons charge. That was a completely different ballgame.

When someone is arrested on a weapons charge, he then is considered a violent felon. Not good at all! The police took him to the county jail. He called us from the police station and told us that he had been arrested and taken to jail. His father and I had to go to his apartment and finish packing his stuff. We drove his truck home and parked it in our driveway. If that was not rock bottom, then I do not know what rock bottom is. Obviously, neither did my son.

Earlier, I mentioned that an addict should never stop celebrating his or her sobriety. I truly mean that. On Facebook, some of the kids who ran with my son back in 2010 will post on Facebook "it has been two years," "it has been three years," etc. I think that is crucial. Unfortunately, my son was too ashamed of his addiction.

Addicts of any kind, no matter their drug of choice, should celebrate the anniversary of their sobriety. Never pretend that your addiction did not exist. It is always going to be a problem and a temptation. Whenever an addict lets his guard down, the addiction bites him in the ass.

One time my son called someone he thought was a friend and said he was clean. The friend's response was, "How long?"

Whether it is a year, a day, or five minutes, it is a blessing for an addict to be clean. That is why they say; take it day by day, minute by minute, second by second.

# GOOD GOD, WHAT NEXT?

On November 3, 2010, my husband and I had to travel to New Jersey. My husband was picking up a car for his job, so I had to go with him to pick up his new car and drive our car back. We got up early in the morning, and my husband went to get some identification out of our lockbox. He needed a passport and birth certificate. He opened the lockbox and said to me, "Your jewelry is gone."

We had to get to New Jersey at a certain time; this was a new job for my husband. My son was upstairs.

I yelled upstairs to him, "Did you take my jewelry?"

He came downstairs with a shocked look on his face. I had caught him. I knew he had taken my jewelry and, yes, it was precious to me, things that had been given to me by my mother and husband. Some of those items were very valuable, both personally and monetarily. I often wonder how long the jewelry had actually been gone.

My husband and I had to leave right away. I broke my own rule, and we left before I could address the theft with my son. Talk about stress. Talk about heartbreak. I knew that to take those precious items from me, he had to be in a very bad way.

We drove to New Jersey, picked up the car, and I sat in the lobby like a zombie, waiting for my husband to finish with his new boss. As usual, I acted like nothing had happened. I had gotten very good at that. I got in the car. He got in his car. We drove back home in about three and a half hours, and naturally my son was gone. I had no idea where he had gone, but I knew about a few possibilities.

# OFF TO THE POLICE

That following Saturday, November 6, I decided that my son needed to be arrested. I would press charges. Enough was enough, and he needed to be held accountable for the jewelry theft. That was the only way to save him. I said to my husband, "I will do this on my own." I went down to the police station and told them the story. I had a list of the jewelry that had been in the lockbox. I told them about my son's addiction and that I was sure he and his friends took the jewelry.

There were other officers standing in the room listening to me. I mentioned my decision to press charges "had nothing to do with the money."

One officer asked, "Were there other people in your house at the time the jewelry was stolen?"

"Yes, of course, there were other people in the house, on and off." We did not even know how long the jewelry had been gone.

The officer said, "Well, if there were other people in the house, you can't prove that your son took this jewelry, with people coming in and out of the house."

Then I made a mistake. I said, "Hey guys, this jewelry was worth a lot of money."

One of the officers in the back said, "I thought you said it had nothing to do with the money."

I had been shot down. They did not have the slightest clue what was going on or what I was trying to tell them. After my futile attempt to do the right thing, I realized I had to find out where my son was.

I knew some of the areas where his friends lived, and lo and behold, I found his truck parked outside one of their houses.

I had cosigned the loan on this truck in 2007, when he was clean. It was around the time my father was dying; I was not thinking clearly. I know I am an asshole. Yeah, he was clean, but relapse is part of the disease. I went knocking on his friend's front door, but no one answered. I sat in my car on a rainy day and wrote a note to him that said he had better come out of hiding, I knew where his truck was, and I had better hear from him soon. I left the note on his windshield. The next day, he called me. He said he was detoxing at his friend's house, all on his own.

I found out after his death that he had gone to detox at one point, but he was turned down. His form from the detox facility stated that he did not qualify and that he "should treat his symptoms as if he had a bad cold or a bad case of the flu." It also stated, "that he should go to the Department of Social Services and apply for Medicaid. Then contact one of the rehab facilities and try to be admitted." This is what I think happened: when we found that the jewelry was gone, we did not know how long it had been missing. I think it had been gone a while, and he was trying to stay clean. He did not qualify for detox, because he was not using enough dope. What could he do? He had to use. Talk about a catch-22.

Remember, an addict must be actively using to get into detox. Hopefully that has changed, but I don't think so. You cannot just go there and say that you feel like using. My son had to do what every junkie has to do in order to get into detox, as sad as that sounds. I think he went out and shot up after the initial refusal in order to get in.

# INSURANCE

Many times my son and I sat at the Department of Social Services (DSS) trying to get Medicaid for him so that he could get into a program. It was not an easy task. There was a time you could go to a particular person at DSS and get emergency Medicaid to get into a program. We had done that twice and then taken him to the program. Several years later my husband and I received a whopper of a bill, which said he had never had insurance.

I had to convince these people that seven years earlier a woman from DSS, no longer there, told my son he could get into the program and that the Medicaid representative would take care of getting the proper information. The representative did see him, but in the shuffle of papers, his records were lost. From what I have been told there is no longer an emergency Medicaid program for addicts.

I made many phone calls regarding this incident. I received many notices from lawyers, courts, utility companies, the IRS, and unemployment, etc. I had to fax a death certificate to them to prove he was dead. I carried his death certificate for two years.

# MEETINGS

At one time, we ran the meeting circuit. Every night after work, I would take him to a meeting, and he seemed strong and focused. This was at the end of 2010. He would not drive the truck, which we had gotten back, so it remained in the driveway. He said something was wrong with the brakes, and they needed to be replaced. It did make an awful grinding noise, which must have been his back brake calipers. I knew he could fix it. He could pretty much fix anything.

The meetings were held in the basements of Methodist or Lutheran churches. He had a regular schedule, and he made a few friends; they were also trying to maintain their sobriety. NA meetings at this time seemed to be a better support group than they had in the past. One of the meetings was even at the court-mandated program that he had been in years earlier. The meetings went on for quite some time, and he did well. He still did not have a job, but now his job was recovery.

Once I picked him up after a meeting; he got in the car and was visibly upset. I asked him why. He told me about the man who had organized this particular meeting for ten years. Most of the meeting leaders had been sober for a long time. This particular meeting had been led in the past by a man who had been clean for ten years. My son found it odd that the he was not there that night, because he was always there. My son asked an old timer where he was. He started to cry and said the man had relapsed. My son was very upset, and so was I. Hope is something that becomes very fragile over time, especially for the addict. This was not a comfortable realization that after ten years a person could feel in his mind, that relapse was an answer, to anything.

# STUPID IS AS STUPID DOES

My son met a girl in the summer of 2010; he did not tell me how. After my son's death, a recovering friend of his told me that, "regrettably," he had been responsible for introducing them. My son hoped she would give him a chance since he was in recovery. Come to find out, so was she. She had used heroin.

He brought her over to the house one night, and I had to give her a chance. After all, my son had the same disease. Who was I to judge her? Also, she was more than a nice girl.

She seemed like a lovely young woman. They were both clean, and I relished that thought. I was not concerned about how long they had been clean; I just concentrated on the fact that they were clean. That pacified me.

Their relationship went fast and furious. She told me more than once that she would never let anything jeopardize her sobriety.

The next thing I knew, he was moving into her apartment. I did not have enough time to think about it. It happened so fast, and neither of them asked me what I thought about the idea. Her family was well aware of the fact that he was a recovering addict, and they certainly were aware that she was a recovering addict. The problem was that I only knew what I, was being told. Her family knew much more about her recovery than I did.

She let me know several times that her family did not approve of their relationship. Only after his death did I find out why (which I will explain later).

When they first started to date, I received a phone call one night from her mother. She sounded panicky and alarmed that these two were together. I did not know what she wanted me to do. These were grown people, recovering addicts yes, but still they were adults.

I had learned a long time ago that telling somebody not to do something was not necessarily going to work.

# LIARS, THIEVES, AND MORE ADDICTS

One thing that bothered me about this relationship was that my son stopped going to meetings. I knew that was not good. They told me that they attended together on occasion. They went back and forth from our house to her grandparents' house. My son became very fond of her grandparents. He and his girlfriend also often visited her brother's house, and her sister would be there with her fiancé. It all seemed to fit just right at the time; he was living with his girlfriend, and she had a decent job.

As a matter of fact, one of the addicts that knew her at that time that she started to use did not understand how she was able to keep that job.

I knew it would become an issue that he did not have a job. She was footing the bill for everything. One afternoon I came home from work; my son had to be somewhere. He had her car, but she desperately needed to pick up a prescription at her doctor's office, just north of us. I offered to take her, and she made it very clear that we had to hurry because she wanted to get there before the office closed. I raced to her doctor's office; she ran in, got her prescription, got back in the car, and we went to the pharmacy to fill her prescription.

It was for Xanax, and I asked her, "Does your doctor know that you're a recovering addict?" She kind of skirted the question. I was confused to say the least.

I know how addictive Xanax is, and it dawned on me afterward that, no, her doctor did not know she was a recovering addict. My son and I talked about it, and he expressed his concern too. I do not think his concern was that she was taking Xanax; I think he wanted to take the Xanax. When that kind of drug was around, he wanted to take it.

She told me in 2011 how great it felt to enjoy a summer because she'd had spent most of the previous summer in rehab. I have no explanation for why I believed anything I was told. I guess I desperately wanted to believe in something.

# Rock Bottom (Again)

It was February 2011, and everything seemed to be okay, for the most part. January came and went without any hassles. My son was cleaning up legal hassles from his last relapse. He had fixed the brakes on his truck and had it up and running. He started a new job, one that his father found for him.

That was also the month my son bounced into my office and announced that he was engaged. I was, to say the least, shocked. He was so excited and appeared to be so happy.

One of the girls in my office said, "Oh, that's great, this will be good for him."

I said, "Yeah, I don't know if that's such a good thing."

One of my other coworkers heard me, and said under her breath, "Yeah, I kind of agree with you, I don't think it's a good idea either."

I did not have a computer back then, so I did not realize that his girlfriend had announced the engagement on Facebook.

My son could tell by the look on my face that I was shocked. "Aren't you happy for me?" he asked.

*No, not really*, I thought to myself.

I do not know how it happened, but he relapsed. By March, he was not showing up to work and did not look very good. He lost the job. That was around the time of the perplexing ER report (see "Falling Out").

# STUPID ME

I did feel bad for the girlfriend at one point. I wondered if she were trying to keep him clean all by herself. I did not know that he was arrested several times during that period. I found all the arrest reports and tickets when we cleaned out his room in February 2014. The police issued him tickets for: being passed out in his car in a parking lot with his keys in the ignition and the truck was running; and for testing positive for all sorts of drugs, when they stopped him on the road. He was a mess.

At one point his girlfriend called me in a panic. She said that my son had her car and had been arrested and she wanted to get money out of her bank account to bail him out of jail. Bailing him out of jail was not something I ever did. If he was in there, he stayed there.

They were not living with us, so I did not have the slightest clue what was happening in their lives. There was a part of me that did not want to know. God forgive me for saying that, but I was tired.

# WHERE IS THE TRUCK?

Sometime at the end of March or the beginning of April 2011, I realized my son was no longer driving his truck.

One day, I asked, "Where is the truck?"

He told me it was in the repair shop. He and his girlfriend stuck to each other like glue, so she was always around. She backed him up no matter what he said.

One day when I was alone with her, I asked where the truck was. She told me the same thing, that it was "being repaired." A "friend" was fixing it because something was wrong with the gas tank. The truck was in my name, I was responsible for it, and I was paying more than $400 every month for it. The charade went on for months. I kept asking where the truck was, and he kept giving me the same stupid answer.

Finally, I said to her, "Come on, his truck is not in the repair shop. If his truck needed to be repaired, he would have pulled it apart in our driveway and fixed it."

I had to find the truck. I could not pay for it anymore. I had paid off all my credit cards with the money I inherited from my parents. Now I had run them up again, trying to keep up with his bills and the car expenses. His father had no idea that I was doing this.

I suspected my son had lost his license. He loved that truck, and I felt badly about having it repossessed, but it was my only choice. I called the bank to advise them of the situation and that I needed to find the truck so that they could repossess it. The search started, and I did not know where to start but thought it probably had been impounded and was in storage at some facility.

I called the police station where his last arrest had taken place. The officer said, "Well, he is in jail, right?"

I said, "No, he is not in jail. I just saw him the other day."

He said, "You have got to be kidding me. We just arrested him and put him in jail. I was trying to get him off the streets."

I did not know my son had been arrested. I told the officer that his girlfriend must have bailed him out again. The officer advised me to call the district attorney's office and speak to a woman who was handling his case. I thought, *What case?* After multiple phone conversations, I finally reached the right person. I found that the truck had been impounded and had been sitting at the city's impound lot for months.

I called the lot, and the man said, "Thank God. Get this truck out of here. It's been sitting here for three months."

Luckily, I did not have to pay a daily charge. I called the bank and gave them the information; then I gave the man at the impound lot the information he needed to arrange to get the truck picked up.

He asked if I wanted "to come by and inspect the truck before it was taken." He said there were "a lot of things" in it.

I did not want to see the truck. I asked my son if he wanted to pick the things up, and he said no. On one hand, I was pissed as hell at him, and on the other hand, I was very sad.

The bank got the truck back on June 29, 2011, my son's thirty-fourth birthday. It was the first birthday of his life I did not spend with him—no conversation, no card, no nothing. I felt like crap, but that is how it played out. That was his last birthday before his death.

# RELAPSE IS PART OF THE DISEASE

Maybe now you can understand why I hate the phrase "relapse is part of the disease." It was a thorn in my side for more years than anyone could possibly imagine. Looking back, I now realize that my son was battling end-stage addiction.

****

Some things that happened throughout my life were due to my own stupidity; however, some situations were no fault of mine. I have lived through a lot over the years, and I am a lot tougher than I sometimes give myself credit for.

One of the girls I worked with told a story about a woman who lived down the street. This woman's heroin-addict son lived with her. My coworker said everyone in the neighborhood was aware of it, even his mother. She wondered why the mother allowed this boy to live in the house when she knew he is a heroin addict.

Years later, I realized I had become that woman with the heroin-addict son. It was not willingly or knowingly, but I became that woman. Oh my God! I knew he was a heroin addict, and yet I could not cast him aside. I guess I understood right from the beginning that my son was a good soul with a very bad disease, and I could not abandon him. Too many people had abandoned him, and I felt bad that he had lost the ability to live a normal life. I got it! I knew why that woman let her son stay with her. He was her son, and she loved him.

# Outpatient

When my son first started outpatient counseling, around 1998, I used to drive him to his appointments and wait for him in the waiting room. At that time, he was seeing a counselor who was a recovering heroin addict. I can still remember his name. His counselor, who was maybe in his late thirties, was blond and blue-eyed, and he looked a little frazzled and beat up by life. You could tell that he had suffered the consequences of his own addiction. The counselor asked my son if his mother was with him. My son stepped into the waiting room, and there I was, sitting patiently as always. My son said, "Yes, she is." His counselor asked him to send me in and sit in the waiting room.

He told me briefly about his own battle with heroin addiction and that my son reminded him very much of himself. My son was like "a snowball in hell," he said. "He doesn't stand a chance if he remains in this area."

Those were his exact words; they ring in my ears and memory to this very day and probably will until the day I die. I was shocked, to say the least, and I thought to myself, *God only knows what he and my son discussed, but whatever it was, the counselor believed my son needed to get out of the area to survive his addiction.* There was almost urgency to what he said. Of course, at the time, I did not realize exactly what addiction was all about; this was all new to me. I did not know what to do. I thought to myself, *Send him away? Where would I send him?*

The counselor was from another state, and he said he'd recently taken the train home because a relative was sick or had died. Even as he rode the train through his old state, he felt the need to use. It was a trigger for him. It had been years since he had used, but when he was least likely to expect it, that old feeling to use came back.

Talk about people, places, and things: *trigger* is another rehab word. Addicts should definitely stay away from those people, places, and things that trigger a relapse. I was new to this world and had to take it day by day. Little did I know that my son was indeed "a snowball in hell."

The thought of him leaving the area seemed unrealistic at the time. My son was around twenty-one years old, and he certainly was not equipped to be sent off with his bags packed to God knows where. Wrong again. I realize now that my son had all the smarts he needed. If he could deal with the type of people he dealt with on the streets, then he could survive on his own—anywhere. I was the one who was not mentally prepared. One of the biggest regrets I have is when my son came to me when he was a senior and said he wanted to go into the military. I should have let him go.

"No, you have to go to college," I told him. Hindsight is twenty-twenty. That was one of those could-have, would-have, should-have moments.

# END STAGE, FALL 2011

We were losing him, and I felt completely helpless. He asked if he could stay at our house for a while. It was obvious that all was not well with his girlfriend. I did not have a computer, so I could not follow what was happening on Facebook. Some of his friends were telling me that they were not getting along. He retreated to his room upstairs, and there was not much conversation between us. The summer came and went, and we were heading into fall. Then the next thing I knew, he moved back in with her.

Then he told us that he and his girlfriend were moving out of the apartment.

I did not know what was going on, and I did not ask. I had stopped asking questions because I never knew if the answers would be truthful. I did not know if she was moving because she could not pay her bills anymore or what the problem was. We never discussed the truck. He never mentioned the truck.

# JAIL—WHAT A RELIEF

On October 2, 2011, which was a Sunday, my son was helping his girlfriend move. They stopped by our house to see if we had any containers, and then the two of them went to the store to buy some. About an hour and a half later, she walked through our backdoor, crying. My son was not with her. She told us that he had been arrested at the store on a bench warrant. I could tell she was hoping we would bail him out. That was not going to happen.

We get a phone call from my son, who said he had made some kind of a deal with the arresting officer. There was a gun-buyback program in our area. We did not have any guns in the house, but my husband owned a shotgun, and the officer was willing to trade my son for that shotgun. My son actually had the officer speak to his father on the phone about this trade off. My husband told him he would not give up the shotgun, and that was that. My husband and I helped my son's girlfriend finish moving and packing her car. It was one of those numb days. I had a lot of numb days. I often felt like I was on remote control. She was crying. I had not cried in years.

I think she went to stay with her grandparents. I have no idea what her family knew or didn't know. I resigned myself to the fact that I was on the brink and could not do much more. My son called me from jail on October 6 and said they were giving him forty days. He would be out on November 10. I sat down and tried to write him a letter, but every time I read it, I realized I had said the same thing, over and over again, for years. There was no reason to send it. That was the first time I did not visit him while he was in jail. I had a terrible sense of relief that he was there. He would call us, and I would accept the charges. It was always a pleasure talking to him when he was sober.

He advised me that a man came to see him while he was in jail, and they were going to accept him into a court drug program. He had to report to the court and a counselor on a weekly basis. We had tried to get him into this program many years before in another county, but they would not accept him then. I think they felt he would relapse, and since the program was just starting, they did not want him to ruin their statistics.

# The Letter

My son wrote me a letter while he was in jail, and it said all the same things I had heard so many times before. He was going to do it this time, he was done, and he was finished using drugs. He could not live his life like this anymore. He told me that he understood that I was not writing to him because I was at my breaking point. He knew I did not want to hear the same things, over and over again, and he needed to get serious and walk the walk. He said he was "tired of being a shitty son." That broke my heart. I was definitely immune.

I picked my son up on November 10, and he looked great. He always did when he was not using. I took him to report to his counselor, who would also do random drug tests. We took him to and from this program, and he eventually received his thirty-day coin. His father took him to that meeting.

When the program was ready to break for Thanksgiving and Christmas recess, the judge addressed the group: "You have a long break before the next meeting, and I know we're going to lose a few of you. I know this is a bad time of the year."

Little did he know how true that statement would be? The next meeting was not until January 6, and that seemed like a long time away. The holidays were approaching fast, and my son was still with his girlfriend. She had just gotten a promotion at work, and there was a Christmas party at her boss's house on December 16. At first, my son did not want to go, but she insisted, so they got dressed, and off to the party they went.

The next week I got two of the strangest phone calls I have ever received. The first call was from a man with a very authoritative voice. He did not say whom he was or where he was calling from, but he asked if my son were there.

I said, "No, I'm sorry, he's not. Can I take a message?"

He said, "No, that's all right, I'll call back later."

The second call came from a young woman who did identify herself. She said she was from the probation department. She asked if I thought that my son had mental-health issues. She put it to me just like that: "Do you think he has mental-health issues?"

The question startled me. Through all these years of him battling this addiction, nobody had ever asked whether he had mental-health issues. I thought to myself, *Wow, they are finally catching on.* I was very nice to the young woman, but I said with a laugh in my voice, "Wouldn't you have mental-health issues if you had been battling heroin addiction on and off for sixteen years?"

Startled by my response, she said, "Oh my God, I'm so sorry. That is terrible!"

Now I am thinking, *What the hell is going on? Who were these people, and why were they looking for him? Why, after all this time, were they asking me if my son had mental-health issues? No one ever seemed to care before.*

# CAT-SITTING?

My sister-in-law and brother-in-law asked my son and his girlfriend to cat-sit at their house, starting January 3, 2012. I did not think this was a good idea, and I told my son that he and his girlfriend should decline. There were those gut feelings again. Was it just mother's intuition?

Then came the phone call. It was December 21. We were home more because the holidays were approaching. The phone rang and my husband answered it. It was a rep from the fraud department of a credit-card company, who asked if we had just purchased a television with my husband's credit card. My husband replied that we did not, and I thought to myself, *I bet it was our son.* I told my husband to call the person back.

I went to the bottom of the stairs and yelled, "Hey, did you purchase a television with your father's credit card?" My son said he had purchased one for his girlfriend's mother.

*My God, is he going to ruin another Christmas?* Stupid me, I was thinking, *Don't let him out of your sight because he will just run off.* It was four days before Christmas. Our daughter had come back into our lives after being away for two years, and we did not want to ruin our time together. My husband and I decided to wait until after Christmas and then try to find out what was going on. We knew our son had to report to Drug Court on January 6, and we figured we would talk to him and his counselor at that time. We had become so used to this type of chaos.

On December 21, my son wrote something in his journal, which I did not see until April 16, 2014, after his death. I will leave it exactly as it was written. I did not know what to say after reading these words:

Today's date is December 21. It is four days until
Christmas. This will be the fourth Christmas I have

again destroyed. I do not know why or how I continue to do this or hurt myself and everyone around me. I have a problem. But what? Why must I commit such horror against the ones around me? It is as though I hate me so much. I continued to convey my hatred of self by hurting those around me. None of me makes sense. All I do is cause anguish, anger, upset, pain, and disappointment. Everyone is right. She needs to run away as fast as she can. She needs to find a man, a provider, a hero of sorts. Not me. I really feel I was born no good. It is nobody's fault, meaning my mother and my father. Maybe my childhood inbred a hatred or feeling of "my fault," but mostly I feel I was born with a gene that just made me a very bad person. When I look in the mirror, I see someone I would do everything in my power to keep away from those I love and care for. When reality hits, I would kill to keep them safe. Here it is I who am to kill the Killer. It is me who I must protect everybody from. Why can I not destroy this demon? Why is it I, who can't make my life right. Why can't I live? Why can't I be human? Why am I such a demon? Why am I such a deviant soul? When will it ever end? When will this pain disappear? I feel it never will. I feel I will never amount to anything. I cannot do anything to beat this demon. Maybe I don't know. I always thought that everything that happened in my life was supposed to. There was a greater purpose. I was to cure the world. I was to discover and help myself by helping others. I thought maybe someday I could help others by telling them my story, hardships, trials, and tribulations. I think now my greatest impact is my death. It would be my greatest testament. My death will or may open the eyes of others to see how dangerous this life is. How dangerous it is.

# How Dangerous It Is

My son and his girlfriend were at our house for Christmas, along with my daughter and her boyfriend. Everyone pretended to be normal, like nothing bad had ever happened in our lives. This was the last Christmas we had with our son. I took his girlfriend aside one day and asked her to please not go to my sister-in-law's house to cat-sit, but they did go on January 3.

I woke up that morning, and he was gone. I called my son on his cell phone and asked where he was.

He answered, "What do you mean, where am I? I'm over at the house cat-sitting."

The next day, I called him, and his phone went to voicemail. I tried his girlfriend, but her phone was turned off, which sent me into a panic. That evening, I received a strange phone call. I did not recognize the number on the caller ID, but it was his girlfriend. She whispered to call her back at another number. I hardly understood a word she said.

My husband sent his brother over to the house that Wednesday, January 4, to make sure my son was still there. Indeed he was. That was also the day my husband found out more about the credit-card incident. Our son had been using that credit card for quite some time. I am sure the bank had made many calls to our home to verify the charges and that my son had taken those calls and said the charges were legitimate. My son had a more mature-sounding voice than my husband did, and he certainly would have known the answers to the security questions (mother's maiden name, social security number, etc.).

It dawned on me later that my son probably had intercepted the bank statements. They always seemed to come around the sixteenth of the month. He must have been found it very stressful to have to constantly watch for the mail. My husband never checked his statements because he had everything programmed into the computer, and payments were sent automatically. Now we know there is a good reason to do things the old-fashioned way.

Guess what our son gave us for Christmas? A brand-new mailbox with a little yellow lever that popped up when the mailman had been there.

After my son's death, we received the credit-card statements and reviewed the charges; most of them were cash withdrawals and charges for items that he could trade for drugs. We had no clue this was going on. There was something else to think about. If my son had been arrested on October 2, and he was in jail until November 10, who intercepted the October statement? I guess we will never know.

\*\*\*\*

I'd thought his girlfriend was with him that whole time. I tried to call his girlfriend's phone and got no answer. I drove by the house to see if there was any activity. It had snowed lightly, and there were tire tracks in the driveway so I thought everything was okay and that the tracks must were made when the girlfriend took her car to work. That night I got another phone call from her. This time I could understand her more clearly, and she explained she was in the mental-health ward at the hospital because she had "a nervous breakdown." *What?*

Worried that my son was alone, I left messages on his cell phone. I was panicked, and I said things like, "Please call me back. You're starting to scare me." There was no answer. My husband's brother had gone to his sister's house on Wednesday, and he said my son was okay. The only reason we were letting him stay there until that Friday was because he had to go to drug court and his father planned to confront him about the charges on the card. My son was made aware of that fact by a voicemail his father left for him on January 4. I do not know what kind of message his father left, but I am sure it was not nice. I kept calling him frantically; I did not know if his phone needed a charge or what the hell was happening. Now I ask myself why I let him stay in that house, especially if he was alone?

The next morning, I drove by the house, and again there were tire tracks in the driveway. It had snowed lightly the night before. I felt that was a good sign—at least there was some activity—but I continued to try to reach him. My husband went to the house on January 5 and knocked on the door, and there was no answer. He figured that our son was either not answering the door or was out on a run. That is a term I always used, a run, was when he was out scoring a bag of dope.

On January 6, 2012, we took my brother-in-law to dinner for his birthday. My husband had been in touch with the counselor and learned that our son did not go to Drug Court that day. I do not know how I made it through that dinner. After dinner, I asked my husband to stop at the house so that we could check it out and talk to our son. We got out of the car and walked around the house. My husband had told me the same lights had been on when he checked the day before. We checked every window and every door, and the house was locked up like Fort Knox. I realize now that we should have broken in, but we were reluctant because of our relationship, or lack thereof, with my sister-in-law and brother-in-law.

As we walked around the outside of the house, I kept saying, "I know he's dead in that house."

My husband kept repeating, "Stop saying that," but I knew we had a problem. Although I knew there was something terribly wrong, it was something I did not want to face. I had become an avoider. I hoped it was just a case of him not getting to his program. It would not have been the first time he skipped a court appearance.

By Saturday, January 7, we knew we had to find our son. My husband went to the house and reported that nothing had changed; the same lights were on, the same fan was spinning, and the house was still locked up. I called my son's last "running partner" and asked him where my son was.

He said, "What do you mean, he's cat-sitting at the house."

"Okay," I said and hung up the phone.

My husband called our local police station, and the officers told us they could not check the house because it was not in their jurisdiction. My husband then called the police for that town. They put a trace on my son's phone, which confirmed that the last call he had made was from that house. The police agreed to meet a locksmith and my husband there. The locksmith opened the door. The police told my husband to wait outside until they checked things out. I was too scared to go.

The police came out and told my husband, "Yes, he is in there."

Shortly after that, my husband came running into our house, crying hysterically. "Yes, our baby is gone!"

I ran to the car, and we drove over to my sister-in law's house, which is about three miles away. We were instructed to "wait outside until the coroner is done." I have to admit, I was in shock. The coroner ran an EKG strip on my son, and he had flatlined. He pronounced my son dead. That was the protocol, even though his body was lifeless and cold.

While I sat in the car waiting for the coroner to allow us into the house, I called his girlfriend at her grandparents' house. Her grandfather answered the phone, and I asked to speak to her. I could tell he was annoyed by my phone call, and he said to me, "She just got out of the hospital."

I said, "He is dead."

Immediately he said, "Oh my God. Oh my God."

My son's girlfriend grabbed the phone out of his hand, and I told her my son was dead. Since his sister and her husband were away, my husband called his brother-in-law's father, told him what was going on, and asked him to please come over. We didn't want to be responsible for their house.

Naturally, I was hysterical. All my nightmares had come true. Once the coroner finished, one of the young police officers said to me, "Ma'am, I don't think you want to go in there."

I said, "I have to. He is my son."

# THE REAL REALITY

We went in through the garage door, walked up the stairs, and there on the couch sat my dead son. It was obvious that he had been dead for a while. My husband and I were living our worst nightmare. I went over to my lifeless son and kissed his cheek. My heart was broken. A bowl of cereal was half-dumped onto his lap. I picked up the bowl and put it in the sink. I was on automatic pilot. I was past the point of knowing what to do or how to do it anymore.

The police officer said, "He [left] a note. Do you want to read it?" I said yes, and this is what it said:

> If by chance, I am not to awaken this a.m., January 6, it was by my own accord. I can no longer destroy those around me whom I love and care for. If only I could have learned to love me. I am so sorry for all the pain and disappointment I have caused. All I have stolen, material as well as spiritual. I am a failure in life, and refused to kill and be killed slowly. I love you all and know in your hearts that I am now safe and free from the jaws of this disease. Mom and Dad, I love you. Please don't let my life be for nothing. Aunt _____, I am sorry for doing this in your home, but I felt very comfortable and a beautiful pathway lay beyond your doors. To all my friends, real friends, I love you, _____, _____, _____, and _____.

He addressed the rest to his girlfriend:

> You will always be my doe-eyed beauty. You are far too beautiful and remarkable for this hell. Love yourself,

your family, your friends. I am so sorry I destroyed our dream and desire. In another universe, we will be together. Until then, always be happy, smile, find love, have a family, and when you look in the mirror, I will be standing beside you, hands on your shoulders, carrying you if you can't walk. You will always be my true love, my one and only. I love you baby.

His last words were:

Please don't cry for me! I will be well and know I am no coward for taking the "easy way out"; I am a warrior. Such as the Japanese samurai who would not die slowly … I offer my soul to the light! I love you all! Until then, [he wrote his name]—1/5/12 11:40 p.m.

# I Am Numb

After his body was discovered, our lives were in complete chaos. I called his last running partner. He and my son were like brothers. My husband made all the appropriate phone calls to tell people that he was gone. The word seemed to spread like wildfire.

Many people felt grief and tremendous guilt for having abandoned him. His girlfriend showed up at our house immediately, grieving terribly, and I honestly felt very bad for her. Plans were set in motion; we bought a cemetery plot and went to the funeral home to make arrangements. The big problem was that we had to wait for the coroner's office to release his body; because it was an unnatural death, they had to complete an autopsy. I did not get the coroner's report until months later. I had to request the report. I felt like my arm had been cut off, and a piece of me was missing. I knew when I had seen his body at the house that he was not there anymore. Only a shell remained; he was gone.

Some days later his girlfriend came to the house and said that during the December 16 Christmas party at her boss's house, my son had been caught looking in the closet for money. She told us this like it was a confession. Her boss went to her and said, "Your boyfriend is a scumbag," as my son ran out the front door.

Looking back, I believe it was a very inappropriate time to tell us about this incident. I am sure that the manner in which she told us, almost blurting it out to get it off her chest, was because she felt guilty. She must have realized she should have let us know he was in such bad shape. We were shocked. No wonder I got those two phone calls from the authoritative man and the girl from probation who asked me if he had mental-health issues. Putting two and two together, I realized they were calling after that event.

The second night after my son's death, one of his friends—the son of his last boss, the one who brought him up on charges for stealing and sexual harassment—came to our house. He and my son had been good friends. He was a mess. He cried in my arms and repeated, "I'm so sorry. I'm so sorry. I'm so sorry." I never asked him what he was so sorry about. I just let it be.

As this young man cried, the lights in the kitchen kept flickering. Oh yes, my son very often gave us what they call "winks." There were all sorts of knocking sounds and unexplainable things. Many people witnessed these winks. The lights flashed in our dining room for many months after his passing. But I did not find comfort in them.

We waited for the coroner's office to release his body on January 10. We were on remote control. His girlfriend remained with us on and off through this time. She was a mess, and I understood why, but I did not pay much attention to her; she was just there. I was too much of a mess myself, as was the rest of my family. People stopped by with things to eat before the funeral took place, and I never really thanked them.

At one point in time, his girlfriend's mother called me to find out how she was doing, and she asked a very strange question. "Do you love her?"

I replied, "Of course we love her."

Her response was, "You do?"

I was not thinking clearly at all, but I thought it was a strange question to ask at a very inappropriate time.

\*\*\*\*

On the fateful day we found his body, my husband took my son's cell phone. We did not know how to use it, and we did not know what his password was. We were in our kitchen before his funeral, trying to figure out how to get into his phone. By mistake, we pushed a button that showed my son had searched the Internet for information on how to commit painless suicide with Temazepam. What the hell was that? We went to my husband's computer and learned that Temazepam is the generic form of Restoril, a sleeping pill. I was familiar with this medication but only knew its brand name. Unfortunately, my sister-in-law had left a bottle of Restoril in her house. My son found the tablets and took them, along with some Darvon she also must have had. Two types of medications were listed on the coroner's report as the primary causes of his death. I do not know the extent of the medications he took. I read the report but did not absorb it. All I remember is that it was not from a bad bag of dope and it was not accidental. The police had said there were empty pill bottles. It was not an accidental death. My son committed suicide, and in my heart of hearts, I realized he probably tried to do so many times.

****

As I mentioned, my family relationships were strained. My husband called my cousin, who then called my sister and told her that my son was dead. Two days after he died, my sister called and asked if her family could come to the funeral. Without hesitation, my husband said yes. Naturally, my sister was distraught. She loved my son. No matter what had happened in the past, this was neither the time nor the place to hold grudges. My son would not have wanted that.

# THE WAKE

How ironic that my son's wake took place on Friday the thirteenth. It almost felt as if he'd planned it that way.

His girlfriend's family were very focused on her, unusually so. Of course she was grieving terribly, so I just put that aside. I was grieving so much that I did not even realize there was a line of people wrapped around the building. Everyone—aunts, uncles, new friends, old friends—was there. All of my friends from work came. My son's old girlfriends were there. They periodically got up to talk to the people they had known through him as they came through the line.

Old running partners, new running partners, recovering addicts— you name it, they were all there. One of my son's old running partners, who had been clean for more than a year, put his one-year coin in the coffin with my son. The crying that day was unbelievable.

Just a few weeks before he took his life, my son had said to me, "Mom, I have no friends." I knew that was not true, but that was how he felt.

Then he asked, "Mom, am I good looking?" That broke my heart. He was so broken. I should have known.

At one point, I looked over, and there in the first row of chairs was his most recent running partner, sobbing and obviously very distraught. I knew he was probably high, but at that point, it did not seem to matter. I felt great concern for him. Although they were not good for each other, they loved each other dearly, and they had their pain in common. It saddened me to see him like that.

The wake was just gruesome. I could not wait for it to be over. The line went on and on for what seemed like forever. One girl introduced herself to me. I did not recognize her name and still do not remember who she was, but she said to me, "Your son was the only person who was ever nice to me in high school."

That took me back a bit, but I needed to hear that. That was my son, the one I knew. Those simple words made me recall what a compassionate young man he could be. I remembered that young man so well. Addiction took him away. I do not remember much about the wake, but I do remember that girl. I want to thank her and let her know how much her words meant to me.

As the funeral home cleared out, I noticed my son's first running partner sitting in the back row. *Oh my God*, I thought to myself. I had not seen him in years. I was not even sure how many years it had been.

I approached him and said, "Why didn't you come up and say something? I didn't even know you were here."

He explained that he "didn't want to interrupt."

I gave him a hug. I mean, after all, he had been a friend of my son's for years. I guess some would call me a fool, but that is my nature. I realize now that he sat in the back, watching the wake like it was a spectator sport. This boy had been through hell and back because he suffered from the same disease and the repercussions. I realized I had to give up any animosity I had toward this person. Back in the day when he and my son were running partners, there was an ongoing battle between our families over who caused who to become such a hopeless drug addict. They were both responsible for themselves, I realize now. He mentioned that he might stop by sometime, and I said that was okay.

# THE FUNERAL

Saturday, January 14, 2012, was the day I dreaded, the day we had to put our son into the ground. I wondered who would deliver the eulogy. The funeral director assured me he had a list of priests, and that there would be no problem. We did not having the service at a church since we were not affiliated with any of the churches in the area. I had been raised Catholic and went to parochial schools all my life, but I had no longer had any connection with the church. You could say I'd lost my religion.

A very nice young priest from a nearby parish gave the eulogy. I asked to speak with him before he started. He came into a room with my family, and we closed the door. I showed him my son's suicide note. As a Catholic, I'd been taught that suicide was a mortal sin.

He read the note. After he finished, I said to him, "Father, when I was going to school, we were taught that this was a mortal sin."

He looked at me and said, "I realize your son was in great pain, and so does God. He has accepted your son with open arms."

There was such comfort in his words. This priest delivered a beautiful eulogy. Then we went to the cemetery to place our son's body into the ground.

Everyone came back to our house and my husband's family was kind enough to bring the food, set it up, and take care of the preparations. I do not remember a thing. They cleaned everything up, and everybody was gone within a couple of hours. I was in shock, numb.

\*\*\*\*

My son's girlfriend spent time with us on and off after the funeral. I felt very bad for her. I knew she was devastated by his death. One day we were all standing in my kitchen, and I asked why she did not have her phone. She said she could not pay the bill anymore. That sounded reasonable since she probably had been footing the bill for all of my son's heroin, which is probably why they had to move out of her apartment.

My husband said, "Why don't you take his phone? That way, we can call you and you can call us."

My son's girlfriend continued to come and go from our house. Sometimes she spent the night up in his room. There were times when she looked very sad and depressed. Many times, she would call and say she was coming over and not show up. I did not think anything about it. Why would anyone want to hang around with us? The grief in our house was so thick you could cut it with a knife.

# THE VISIT

I was downstairs one night, wearing my robe. It was February 13, 2012, and someone knocked at our door. It was dark so I could not see who it was. I opened the door, and there stood my son's first running partner. My husband knew he was coming; I did not. We asked him to sit down, and we started to talk. I was not quite sure about the purpose of the visit.

He asked me questions. "Why do you think he killed himself?"

I said, "I don't think he could handle the guilt anymore." I believed my son had gotten to the point where his conscience bothered him.

This young man looked at me and said, "Well, that's not one of my problems."

I thought to myself, *Well, aren't you lucky that your conscience doesn't bother you.*

Then he said to me, "I thought he was doing well. What happened to him?"

He told me about an incident that took place many years ago, when he was clean and my son was not. My son went to his friend's workplace and took money out of the register. This was a story I had heard before. I think his girlfriend at the time told me about it and that she had to pay back the money. He referred to my son as a scumbag and when he saw the expression on my face, he said, "Well, I guess I was a scumbag, too."

I was totally shocked by the things he was saying. I expected to hear sentiments like "I'm so sorry we ever started with heroin." But that is not how it went. He was not comforting at all. At one point, I got up and went into the kitchen, as I was getting antsy. He followed me, leaned over my kitchen counter and said, "Are you at the point where you're relieved yet?"

I said to him, "Are you kidding me? I loved my son. There is no relief in his death for me. I did everything I could to keep him alive!"

Then he said, "Why did you let him come back in the house?"

I replied without even thinking: "Because I didn't want him to die on the street."

His friend left shortly after that. He could tell I was a little upset, to say the least. This was only February 13, and here he was asking me questions like that. His lack of sensitivity shocked me.

My husband said, "I guess you forgot that he never really was a very sensitive young man." Well, he certainly reminded me.

# THE BIGGEST LOSS OF ALL

I have gone through so many stages since my son died. I miss him terribly, and there are times when I can hardly bear to exist. I see pictures of him scattered around the house. I look at this boy's face and wonder how this could have happened. As I have stated before, he did not have the face of a heroin addict. What does a heroin addict look like? Look in the mirror. Few people realize how life-threatening addiction can be unless they experience it. It has been a rotten learning experience.

I have experienced addiction up close. I realized from watching it year after year that there is great pain involved. The addict is anesthetizing the pain they cause themselves and the pain they inflict on others. Reverse psychology does not work, so do not bother. Addiction seems to heighten users' sensitivity levels, and they do not take criticism well.

I always tried to let him off the hook by saying, "Hey look, I've made mistakes, and the only way I can redeem myself is if I say I'm not going to do it again, I don't do it again." Sounds simple doesn't it? It is simple to someone who has his or her head on straight.

These are all side effects of this drug. That is not an excuse. That is a fact.

# ANGER

I am angry that our health system does not do more to help the addict with mental-health issues. I am angry that addicts are not accepted into detox unless they are high. I am angry that heroin causes such hopelessness and helplessness among addicts and their families. I am angry that you need insurance to get into a decent program. I am angry with myself and the powers that be for not recognizing my son's mental status.

I think I knew him well as he was growing up. He was so honest in his thinking and feelings and how he felt about his friends. These people were important to him; yet this drug alienated him from every single person he loved, and he knew it. I am mad that my son felt so much helplessness and hopelessness that he could no longer foresee a future for himself.

I am mad that my son took his own life.

# Jail 2009

My son started writing a book during one of his stays in jail in 2009. He describes how he found heroin, or rather, how heroin found him. This chapter is actually my son's book, which was given to me by his girlfriend after his death. It had been under his nightstand.

Please remember that this was written three years before he passed. I was not aware that he had written this account of his life with addiction. The first time you read this will be the first time for me also. I have not had the heart to sit down and read his words before this.

After a while, sounds become second nature. They do not seem to enhance the surroundings any longer as they used to. All the senses seem to diminish. No longer do you hear the clanks of the steel on steel when they collide in the fluid manner all too familiar. No longer do the whines of motors, which drive these structures, rumble your eardrum. The feeling of pale flesh to concrete and steel, which at one time sent a chill to the bone, is now a blanket of security. No color, no smells, no taste. Repetition is deadening, almost destructive. Yet when you have stepped foot in as many hell holes as I, like this, it all becomes almost comforting, so real. The fluorescent lights cast strange shadows on things. Not that there are many shapes, nor things to catch the light, but what is there certainly radiates what it can. Silver, gray, white, tan, that is all I see. The little light my window lets through transforms the colors to blahhh. Outside are asphalt, fence, wire, and brick. I am truly in the pen like an animal that has been bad. However, maybe that is exactly what I am?

Have you ever just sat and watched nature? For instance, an ant. A tiny creature that seems to dart from place to place along the ground. No particular path, no particular destination. Yet, that ant has a purpose. Part of a greater plan. Part of something bigger.

I sit here now amongst the worst of the worst, in my bland, washed-out existence, and can only pray. That I, like the ant, am part of the bigger plan.

Do not ever let anyone tell you the life of the junkie, whether active or not, is easy. I know firsthand, for I am a junkie in the perfect definition. The first time I pierced my flesh by my own accord and pumped that juice directly into my bloodstream, I started a fire that would rule my existence for almost 13 years. In a lifetime, 13 years might seem like nothing. For a junkie, 13 years is a lifetime. Never knowing what the next move will be. Where the next hit will come from. I feel I have aged 40 years in 15 years. Not because of what the dope has done to me physically. Unbelievably, most junkies I know looked particularly well for their age. Me as well. I am now 32 and still look 24. No, it has not aged me that way, but let me tell you the lives I have lived, the stories I have heard, the things I have been through and seen, touched, said and done, have aged me. Aged me far greater than the years I have lived. Almost as though I was stuck into a microwave at 16 years old, set on high, and cooked for 15-plus years. Imagine what that would do to [a] frozen dinner.

Somewhere along the line, someone said I should write a book, which I haven't the foggiest idea how to do. I mean, where do I start? Do I try to use my whacked-out sense of humor? Do I try to be scary to make people cringe? I really have no clue how to start. Would people want to read this shit anyways? I cannot see people wanting to depress themselves anymore by reading my stories. With all the shit in the world now, fuck, who would care? Then I figured, why not? Why not share my stories? Maybe I can help someone. Maybe I can change a life. Maybe I am writing this more for me than anyone else. Maybe this is I, at my most selfish. Thinking fuck it, write this and read it every day so I never have to be here again.

I was young when I began experimenting with drugs. As most kids in the early '90s [were], I was a tad confused. The '80s were over, thank God. A hippie movement seemed to start up again. The preppy kids crawled out from under their Lacrosse shirts and polo shirts. The heroin-chic movement was creeping slowly. Music spoke of addiction, trying to beat it and such. If you are a rich kid you could afford a bottle of booze on the weekend and a little pot, or you could always steal it from your parents.

Me, I was quite the entrepreneur at a young age, the salesperson just like my dad, kind of. I would steal bottles of booze from my dad, who himself sold liquor, legally, of course, and sell the bottles for 20 bucks to the kids who could afford it, which seemed like everybody in my posh school. I never really drank much. I had a few little experiences, but not a drunk. I guess my criminal activity started before heavy drug use, kid stuff, at least I thought. I was arrested for breaking into a car, stupid shit, yet wrong. I was raised better than that. I knew that but that was part of the problem. I wanted to experience that being wrong feeling, and so I did.

Around that time I had fallen for a girl; she happened to be one of the popular girls in school—perfect! We hit it off well, me skater kid, pack of cigs, chain wallet, big pants, and sneakers. She was a preppy girl. What a combo she and I soon became. I would soon be preppy, and we would smoke together around '91.

We started dating, skipping classes, and taking off to smoke cigarettes off school grounds. You see my parents were smokers, not cigs, but pot. It never had the same effect on them as it did on me. The first night I really remember smoking, I only remember laughing my ass off all night and having a great time. She and I smoked every day. Our favorite thing would be to smoke before sunset, put on some music and lie in my bed, and watch the stars. I had thousands of stickup, glow-in-the-dark stars, which I stuck on my ceiling.

I met many new people, was having a blast. At least I thought. I enjoyed going to shows, jam band stuff. Therefore, at shows, I would take a tab or two of acid, nothing huge, but I loved the openness acid offered me. I never saw myself as an acid freak though. I knew then that was not for me. No, not me! Not this guy! I was doing nothing wrong in my mind by smoking pot. Shit, I was not even a drinker. At the end of 1994 we broke up, high-school shit; we all have been there at one time or another.

It was about this time things slowly evolved for the worse. What does one do when you have a terrible breakup with your high-school sweetheart, your first true love? Well, of course you do what any teenage fool does, surround yourself with friends, meet new ones, and do drugs, lots of them. I met some new friends at this point. One who was later to become my partner in crime, and my running partner.

I had become very hippie at this point. I drove an '81 BMW 320I, covered in stickers, my hair had grown long and shaggy. I made sure to wear worn-out jeans and T-shirts. Boy, was I a sight. I was a perfect match for someone looking to feel less guilty about doing drugs by himself. I would be the perfect target. I had met this person. Also a pot-smoking hippie type, had a great car, with a five ball for a shifter. Orange, beat-up, and just cool. I also palled around with another friend who himself was a cool, hippie, pot-smoking type. There was also the Bee man, who was then and is now my best friend of such, although maybe not right now due to the situation. I still owe him 40 bucks. I took him to one of his first shows June 21, 1999—summer solstice show—so you have me and three other friends that were close and a few others that need no mention, not because they were not cool or anything, but the list could go on forever and ever.

Then that one summer night, he came like a cowboy over the plains searching in the parking lot. I had known this friend in high school. For some odd reason people picked on him very bad; bastards. He was a heavy kid, but all right. He pulled in; I had not seen him in some time. He had lost a lot of weight, yet did not look healthy. He was pale, beads of sweat on his forehead. His eyes were crazy, darting back and forth. His pupils were the size of dinner plates.

We talked briefly, having not seen each other in some time. Then it happens.

"Geez, you lost weight, you look good." I almost hesitated saying it.

That is when I was informed he had a gram of the highest grade of coke on him. "Want to do some with me? Can we go to your place?"

Now I had never really done coke before this. I had now graduated high school, was working full-time, and things were good. I had been accepted to a private school, which thrilled my parents, seeing that my guidance counselor in high school said I did not apply myself. Therefore, I was doomed. I was to begin fall semester, but for now thought, why not? We got to my house, into the computer room, and like a hot iron to my ass, I started talking and asking questions and philosophizing and listening to music and dancing, and did another line. This went on until it was gone at 3 a.m.

I lay awake and thought about 1 million things, but the one thought that would not escape me, was more. I was using coke and a lot of it. He would give me money, and I would go buy coke; by this time we had graduated from a gram a night to a ball, 3.57 grams. A group of us would sit, up and snort coke and imagine ourselves rock stars, ripping lines off an amp during set breaks. All we were was just young, stupid, suburban kids using someone else's money. Downing coke like it was a job. I knew things started to get bad when he would still try to suck the shit through a bloody nose. Gross.

It is hard at times to wash away the memories. You almost want to erase a period of time. For many addicts, they dream of easing the bad memories. The times that make them cringe. That one-night stand, the embarrassing moment at work, the day everyone noticed that you are wearing two different socks.

Things at this point had not been terrible. Well, at least major consequences were not showing their ugly face; not yet! I was attending college. I have always had the gift of gab. I am a very social person by nature. Total type A, much like my father. My personality was a great character trait, but would soon become a weapon to get what I wanted, along with my all-American, good-boy looks. I thought if needed to, I could get away with anything. My teachers liked me. My grades were not terrible at this point, even though I was not really applying myself.

Socially in college, I was doing well. Had a cute college girlfriend and had made friends with others on campus. Everything seemed normal on the outside, so normal that when it happened, not even I knew.

By spring, something had happened. Something had changed. Priority seemed to shift; the skies seemed to darken, even in the bright sun. I did not have the ability to realize things were changing for the worse. I had made friends with a kid on campus. He was quite a character. Super cool, guitar-playing, acid-dropping hippie. We hit it off right away, and it was a place on campus to go smoke pot, and listen to music while he dropped copious amounts of acid and we spoke of other times, the '50s and the '60s. How glorious it would have been to ride the rails through the West, kings and queens. At this point, it was also a place for me to do my share of coke, which at this point I would buy a bit here and there. I spent many nights there in his little room, just off campus. Me and a group of others, just doing coke.

I have always wondered what happens just before you die. Like the guy who puts a gun to his head and pulls the trigger, what is the final thought? Can you smell the powder? Hear the click? The bang?

The only reason I ask is because of what happened next. This is the moment where I redefined my life. I never heard it, saw it coming, or prepared for it, yet can only attribute it to putting a gun to my head and pulling the trigger. A game of Russian roulette that would last for the next 13 years. Today I realize how much slower a death it is than popping my lid off with the .45.

Oh, much slower, so slow in fact, I had no clue what was happening. I had become somewhat disenchanted with the whole coke thing at this time. All of us were becoming a human coke vacuum. On the other hand, we had fun with it, but the staying up late, mixed with coke psychosis. I find that defined by the paranoid looking out the window and seeing someone in the trees and they were always out to get you, and it began to lose its luster.

Friends from my past were noticing, and I had even heard "coke head" being thrown around. It felt good, but the comedown sucked. Then it happened one night.

This is where my friend left, to get a supply of coke and came back half an hour later saying, "I got fuckin beat."

"What? How?" I said. We had all chipped in a couple bucks.

He said, "I gave the guy that 80 bucks, and he gives me these four tiny bags of bullshit. Look," he says, dropping the bags on the worn-out college apartment coffee table. This is where my friend, soon to become running partner, recognized that the bags were not coke, but heroin.

My first running partner said, "That's not coke dude, you didn't get beat; that is heroin."

Still he said, "Oh shit, now what?"

"Can we sniff that?" I asked.

He said, "Of course, but only a tiny bit, that shit can be strong, depending on how good it is. Shit, I wish I had a needle. I saw this guy shoot it once, looked amazing," he said with a disappointed tone.

"Let's do it," I said, and as they say, that is that! He opened one of the small translucent bags stamped with the word Stingray in a faint stamp of what appeared to be didn't matter. Spilled the brownish powder out and split it three ways. One of the guys with us that night was not interested, and I thank God.

We each sniffed a small line of the powder. "Shit burns, taste like yuck. Nasty!" I said.

"That means it is good, right," the fellow who went out to buy it says—he had heard that the more it burns the better.

"Just give it a second, we will see how good it is," says my new running partner. We had a half-dry cough and half-dry heave as the powder disappeared.

I think back to that night and wish that it was one of those memories I could erase. That I could remove that day, that night from my life. I cannot say that if heroin had presented itself to me again if I ever would have tried it, but I had.

For the next 13 years I would play a dangerous game, one like no other. One that would imprison me within the bars of my mind, as well as those man-made. The game that would bring me here today for 13 years. I have danced with the devil.

It really is funny how many people gawk and blink in disbelief when they hear my story. Both fellow inmates and guards will comment, "You do not fit the classic profile of a junkie." Trust me, I know. Although throughout the years, I think the classic profile has changed.

Sure, you have your gutter junkies. These are the ones you picture in your mind. The ones you see on TV and hear about in stories. Tattered clothing, colorless eyes, almost like black holes. Skin red and scabbed from years of rubbing and scratching, picking, and/or lack of washing. I have heard more than one junkie state that they prefer not to shower, due to the fact that they feel that the dope hits them harder. Your gutter junkies live no place in particular. They live everywhere in general, and are found on city streets waiting for the next score.

Then there is the new generation of junkie, I have met. I always try to warn them. They are the suburban kids, young boys and pretty girls, misguided. Not by parents, necessarily, although there are some, but more often than not by friends who first turned us on to the rush of morphine.

We saw and thought that heroin chic look of the mid- and late '90s looked good. Dark circles under the eyes covered by designer shades. We had no clue but thought we knew what we wanted. The wandering got worse, and soon we wandered away from what we knew was right and moral. Family, friends, schools, jobs, and we wandered into a deadly world. Some of us wander forever, until we die or get out. Simple as that.

We do not fit the mold, but we are without a doubt here. All it takes is too long of a dance, playing the song too long, or becoming brave and piercing flesh was surgical steel and tasting the devil's breath directly through your veins.

See, as junkies, we have at one point become dope-sick, a junkie's greatest fear. No junkie likes to see someone sick. It is almost a code to help another out. Even if just the corner of a bagger or cotton, which is dangerous in these days of AIDS and Hepatitis C, yet sometimes it is the only way. Always looking for handouts, pain in the ass, to the nth degree. First, the last words out of your mouth are, "You know I'm sick, got anything?" The best part is when you know, that after a while, we burn every bridge and need to stay sick or quit.

Dealers, now here is an interesting topic. I have met some real fucked-up people out there, but I have never met more fucked-up people than dope dealers. They are the most OCD, paranoid, bipolar, neurotic, switch-artists I have ever met. The dealer who [is] your best friend one day hates you the next. The person who is buying from his cousin on Tuesday is cut off from him on Thursday. They fight on Friday, make up on Saturday and Sunday. All is good. This is expected and a regular routine, no reason to be alarmed. I have run across what I can only figure to be every type [of] dealer out there.

There are a few who can be defined as the classic, my get-high dealers. These dealers really teeter on the dealer scale. They are junkies as well, most often gutter junkies, although sometimes they fall into the wanderer trend like myself because they use. They often do not have dope on them, but they certainly know where to get it. Anytime, anywhere, and anyplace. Although when asked, "You got anything?" their reply is always, "Come with me." If they say they are holding, 95% of the time they are not, or once you get there they've conveniently just sold the last three bags. Those same three bags you were just promised 10 minutes ago and told them to hold onto. See, you are their get-high. This is defined this way—you need them, they need you, a relationship built in harmony. When they do have something, always caution on the side of error. It can, will, or could be tapped, meaning partially emptied as to look like there is dope in the bag, even though it is only half-full. Typically, they would need the money up front, have to run to get it. No, you cannot follow and [they] tell you they will meet you in 10 minutes, even though they mean half an hour. They do their best not to burn you or be obvious about it because, again, without you and others like you, they do not get high. They are willing to get you something whenever, as long as you are getting them one. More often than not, you would have found me with one of them. He would get high off me and my money, yet I was his transportation. Which means when I drove him to take care of others, I was taken care of, a junkie's dream. Kind of?

Next we will examine the Biggen. These guys are the top dogs. Sometimes you know them; more often you do not. You know where they live, what they drive. Maybe you have seen them; then maybe not. Someone you know knows them and will not give up their identity. This is more selfish than a protection for them. No junkie wants to give up the Biggen to another junkie; by doing so you give up your get-high status.

These guys always have dope, never let you come to the house, always meet you in the worst of places, if they will meet you at all, and again, say 10 minutes when they mean 30. The dope is usually good, consistent, and moderately cheap. They always drive a different car and really don't say much on the phone. They use code words, such as T-shirts, CDs, movies, cookies, bags, etc. [An] example would be, "How many T-shirts you need? How many bags you need?" Minutes, beans, chips, girls, dollars, cash, all code words. Okay, give me 60 minutes at CVS and 10. Translation, you need three bags okay, give me $60 at CVS and 30 minutes. Confusing, yes; careful, not really. Unless you are one of those who thinks cops are stupid. Whatever the case, they make big money, more often than not; they like to deal with big quantities. No matter what, they are usually the fastest and best choice when it comes time to buy your junk.

Next, we will examine the sketch. Typically, this dealer is a tad sketchy. Buys a few bundles, 10 bags at a time, and works them until gone. Once it is gone, it is usually gone for some time. Do not ask this dealer for a break. They are not paying much less than what they charge you. Straight money or exact change is all they take. They are sketchy because you never really know a thing about them. Just a phone number and strange names, weird names. Always on foot. Meeting in alleys or bathrooms at fast-food restaurants, places where "we wouldn't be seen." Sometimes these dealers are family guys. People you would not really ever expect would deal. I have met cops that deal, legal aides, nurses, railroad engineers, and even drug counselors that deal. They get rich quick or get a little spending money on the side that is the goal. Again, many of those people are sketchy; maybe because they are so sketched out by us junkies, they reciprocate the feelings.

There was a time when you could cop a bag of dope off the streets, but technology they have put a damper on that. Thank God. Cameras in the trees, informants everywhere and cops on the street have forced many to redefine their business and take it inside, off the streets.

I have just begun to explore the wants, wonders, sadness, sorrow, hates, and activities of the junkie, namely me. This biography of sorts is about my journey, my background. It is my testimony, my story, my life as a junkie. It is the reason I sit here now locked up again thinking and dreaming of the world outside. Which is happening without me? The girlfriend I loved and wanted, forever gone. The trust I rebuilt with others gone, the job, the money, the car. The life I had only months ago, stripped from me like a metal from a juiced-up Olympian. They say everything happens for a reason. I hold on to that, like the last breath I will ever take. I am to believe that this is true for I have no other explanation.

Although I had been doing copious amounts of cocaine in the beginning, heroin brought me down so slowly and carefully, like a mother lays her child into a crib. All the insecurities I had were gone. Do not be fooled. Hell is not always fire and brimstone. With this disease, hell is coming, and wants you to feel welcomed. Very welcome. I closed my eyes in an unknown new abyss, and I faded away.

****

*The Crime Scene*

That next morning after having done heroin for the first time, I remember waking to an empty living room. The hustle and bustle of the evening before was gone. I was alone in the room. Evidence of a small party the night before, swept clean like a sanitized crime scene.

If not for the feeling of nausea, I may have thought I had almost dreamt the whole thing. In an instant, I rose and in a feverish effort made my way to the sliding glass door that led to the deck outside. Sliding the door open and barely making it, I vomited violently.

I remember calling my friend and saying, "What the hell happened last night?" I really could not remember, and my friend reminded me of the whole evening. The party at the college, the beer bongs, some blonde girl, and my friend thinking that he got burned and the fact that I had my first taste of heroin.

I was not sure how I felt about this. I was caught up with the idea that I had used heroin the night before. I reminded myself that I had only sniffed a little and that there was no real reason for me to be alarmed. Or was there?

I grew up in a typical suburban family. My parents were good people. They did all they could to provide for us. It was me and my younger sister. She was six years younger than I was, and as it would turn out, completely different than me. The first years of my life, I remember our duplex, my mom's long blonde hair and thin model frame, and my father's broad shoulders and large frame.

My parents met at the bus stop; my mother was new to the area. My father was born and raised here, which meant my grandparents would wind up living about seven houses apart on the same road. I guess it made things convenient on holidays. At least it should have. My mom was a nurse at the maternity hospital. Around the time of my sister's birth in 1983, my father started a job at a local liquor distributor. I guess my father drank a little too much. Although it is hard to remember specifics.

I always loved my parents very much. Growing up they always had friends over, music playing and danced. They were free people, not hippie as you think hippies, but free and not staunchly and stuck up. I always remember my parents smoking pot. My father would bring bags of it home. When I was old enough to know what it was, I rather resented that they did.

I remember vividly one summer day when I was 12, I told my best friend that my parents smoked pot and that it disturbed me bad. I confessed to him the secret. I remember him telling me it was no big deal.

His older brother did too, and he as well. He was a few years older than I was. Therefore, I guess it made sense. I was relieved that it was more normal than I thought. All we ever heard in those days was, "Just Say No," and America's new war on drugs, and for a child then, thinking your parents were fighting for the wrong side was scary. It should not have been a big deal, I guess.

My mother's sister used to take me up into her bedroom [when I was] as young as seven and we would listen to 8-track tapes, while she would take bong rips. Looking back on it now, no wonder I became a pothead. Again, I just passed it off as growing up in a free family.

I spent a lot of time with my mom's parents every week and I would sleep over, and we would all get together for Sunday dinners. For some reason a rift had started before I was born between my dad and his father. My father was not all too cool with Grandpa. Grandpa was not the most ethical man. Grandpa had a roofing business, and my father worked with him from time to time. This on more than one occasion started problems.

Looking back, I do not know how everything fell apart the way it did. My Gaga and Pop (Mom's mom and dad) had drifted away. I, for years, have tried not to blame myself, but a few fingers point to me. To sum it all up, I didn't have all that much of a fucked-up childhood. Shit happened that sucked but no matter what, and through all the bullshit, there was never an excuse for me to do what I was doing. No reason for me to travel down the road to destruction.

I became someone with a story. I had tried it and fell in love with heroin. Although cunning as it was, I really did not know just how powerful it was yet. At this point, my running partner and I were inseparable.

He began attending the college I went to as well, so we would regularly hang out. He was living with his girlfriend at this point. At first, I was attending classes, and I had met a girl who I was struck by. She was a beautiful brunette and incidentally on the swim team, so she most certainly had a swimmer's body. One day I asked if she wanted to have a drink and chill. Sure enough, she said yes. That was cool. She took my mind off shit for a while. Yet on the weekends, I would get together with my running partner. We would sniff coke and dope and play cards. This was a weekend thing, right? My one friend who was into the coke really did not enjoy the dope. Every time he did it, he would puke. He pretty much stuck to the coke.

\*\*\*\*

*Slow and Easy*

See, the thing about addiction for me was how it happened so slowly. I have heard the stories about the crack smokers who take their first hit and become addicted. For me, it was slow. It seemed as though the heroin did not want me to know exactly what was happening. I noticed something was up, but just could not put my finger on it.

By this point, my little dealer could not keep up with my friend's enormous coke habit, so we found someone else. I honestly do not know if I ever knew his name. I do remember him being a huge black man about six foot four and probably 320 pounds. I never dealt with him but I would go with my running partner to meet him on occasions.

On Fridays, we would split a $20 bag, that was that, 10 bucks apiece. This would last us Friday night, and a bump Saturday midday to carry us to Sunday.

The rest of the week, we would chill, school, girlfriends, and hang out a bit. Then on Friday, it would start again. On more than one occasion, I remember catching myself at the last second before running into a parked car or guardrail. See, one of the effects of heroin is a soft, hazy light, euphoric bliss that brings the mind and body into a dreamlike, sleep-like state.

I am not sure at what point I realized the change. All I knew is that it came. Things start to lose their priority. School and my girlfriend, which sucks because she was really a cool girl. I just faded away with no explanation. Everything changed at work. People noticed the change in me. I was really starting to look a tad raggedy, hair was long and gnarly. I just was not myself.

By this time, we each needed a bag on the weekends, and our use stretched into Thursday. I started to notice that on the days I was not using, things just didn't seem right at all. I began almost feeling sick to my stomach. My skin felt like sandpaper, eyes watered, could not concentrate on anything. Yet when I used, I felt great, normal, cool, collected.

I will never forget the day my mom said, "Wow, you have really mellowed out. I am really proud of you." I remember laughing in an attempt to disguise what she had just said. I almost could not believe it. It was true, I was. Not that I was a wild kid, but now I was really mellow. Still, no one knew. All my friends were clueless, family clueless, employer clueless. People may have speculated, thought I was a pothead or something, but heroin? No way! I had stopped using coke. I just used dope and now it had become Wednesday through Sunday, then Thursday.

Before I knew it, it was too late. I became a full-fledged heroin addict. I mean, I did not think so and certainly would not admit it, but I had. By this point, it was costing me 80 bucks a week to maintain my habit. My running partner as well who was having problems with his girlfriend had decided to move out and get some space.

We just decided to move in together. Bad idea. He had found a little basement apartment in the city and we lived in the ghetto actually. I think I was stopped about four times by the cops, wondering, "What the hell are you doing in this neighborhood?"

"I live here," I would say. I guess they figured I was a college student and it was all we could afford. The apartment, besides being in a city neighborhood, was really nice. New appliances, new carpet, painted and nicely put together. We rented it from a nice couple who lived upstairs. It was cheap, clean and everything we needed and close to school. He got the bedroom. I got the couch, which I did not mind because then I got the TV.

Little did I know this would be the birthplace of my end … and/or beginning?

The first time I actually saw my running partner shoot heroin, I was not sure what to think; it all happened about two weeks before we had to move into a dingy basement apartment. Somewhere along the way, he had purchased an old mahogany case with brass hinges from a flea market or garage sale. When he opened it, there was an old, antique syringe set, with a glass syringe plunger and four very large steel needles. It must have been 100 years old.

Intimidating, yet so intriguing. I would have never imagined using such a device for self-injection. Maybe in 1906. This would do, but by today's standards, this device was outdated, historical, and just looked like it would hurt like hell. Still, for some reason I had to watch.

My running partner knew a guy who had regularly been shooting dope and this invited the temptation for him to do the same. I watched as he poured the contents of the bag into a spoon, added water, touch the bottom of the spoon to a flame from a votive that burned on the makeshift table. There was a slight odor, which erupted into the air, almost like incense. He dropped a small piece of cotton onto the spoon and sucked up some of the brown fluid. He took that monstrosity of ancient medical equipment and drove the smallest of the needle, now attached to the glass syringe. In one motion, he sucked the fluid from the cotton into the glass. I watched with such intensity and concentration. He raised the device, tapping it slightly to work the air from the chamber, pushing the plunger ever so gently until a bubble of the solution shown itself from the tip. He wrapped a piece of surgical tube around his arm. Immediately a vein arose from the surface, and he poked that nail of the needle into his thick skin. Holding the tube in his mouth, you could see him wince and his eyes squint. It just looked like it hurt. A flash of red sprung into the chamber and as fast as it came, it was gone with the solution in the device. He released the tube and sat down. I saw his eyes flutter and heard his breath release and the steady "ahhh ..."

"Well," I said.

"Amazing, absolutely amazing," he said trailing off.

Now that was the first time I saw him shoot dope. I had the feeling he had shot dope before, but I didn't really know. He just looked too cool, calm, and collected while doing so. Whatever the case, it looked good, and I knew it would not be long until I had tried such a thing. I was determined to feel what he felt. Sniffing had lost all its glory, and I thought it was getting expensive. Boy, I had no clue.

I had finished classes and headed to the doctor's office where my grandmother worked. I had developed a nasty wart on my finger. For some reason I had an appointment to have it removed.

"Hey, hi baby," she said as I walked through the door to the window, which framed her perfectly.

"Hi Ga, I'm here for my appointment."

"Sure baby, room two."

I walked into the room and sat down. There was always a little wait. I got right in which was nice, not having to sit in the waiting room thumbing through magazines on health care and interior design books, but there was always a little wait. I remember looking out the window, the sky a sullen gray, overcast. No shadows, the leaves already changing, some falling already. In an instant, my eyes flipped to the cabinets that were right in front of me. Doors, cabinet doors, hmm ... I don't know why I chose to open the one drawer. There in the drawer were about 15 hypodermic syringes of a few assorted sizes. My eyes opened wide as I examined each one, thinking which would be most appropriate. I quickly thought back to the night in that basement and that medieval-looking syringe. Too big, I thought, too small, I thought ... and just like Goldilocks, I thought just right. I grabbed two of the hypos. Stuffed them in my pockets along with a handful of alcohol pads, and sat back down, awaiting the doctor.

My finger stung like hell after the treatment. I rushed into the apartment. I screamed coming through the door. There was no answer. On the table was a note that said he was out with his girlfriend, probably going to grab something to eat. "Not sure when I will be home. Saw him this morning, glad you left that money. You should be all set. If you leave, lock up, if not, see you later."

For some reason he always thought he needed to remind me of everything: lock up, turn off the lights, make sure the fridge is closed. More often than not, I was the one turning off the lights, closing the fridge door, and cleaning up after him. I had left 40 bucks with him that morning. I did not have to work that night, no school, and I had pretty much finished my photography assignment.

I figured I would sit back, relax, and get a little faded. In that same millisecond I remembered that slight bulge in my pocket; reaching in I pulled it out. I knew that was my last stand. Fuck it. I had left 40 bucks and gotten two bags for myself. I thought to myself, let's do this.

I had been sniffing dope a few months. Finally, I had the means, the method, and the mode. I went into the bathroom and turned on the light. I remember standing there staring in the mirror at myself, my mind a dark chasm of dreams and memories. I pulled the hypo out of my pocket, unwrapped it delicately like a surgeon would for a surgery. In a very specific and methodical fashion, I placed the spoon next to the lighter next to the bag next to the hypo. I opened up the bag, pouring it into the spoon. I really was not sure how much I should do. I mean, I had been using a bag a day for a few months, give or take a day. Was there a formula? The last thing I wanted was to be found dead in the bathroom. Three-quarters of the bag should do fine. I pulled water up into the syringe, 25 units, holding it up and inspecting the contents. I slowly squirted it into the spoon with powder and watched them wrestle with each other for a second, the water winning and slowly devouring the powder. I flicked the lighter and touched the flame to the bottom of the spoon lightly, just a little until the solution had time to hiss and bubbled. I put a piece of cotton into the spoon, stuck the needle into the cotton, and sucked up all the liquid. Again, I looked into the syringe, pushed the air out, and thought to myself, Well, you have hit the big time.

I closed my eyes and concentrated on my breathing until it was slow and rhythmic. I was about to, for the first time in my life, shoot heroin into my veins. I hated getting shots! What was I thinking? This was definitely different than getting a shot. This was the ultimate high, the ultimate escape. I was no pussy, no slouch. No, I was going to do this, that lust for life or lack of it. I opened my eyes, tied my arm with a necktie, then slapped my arm. A vein rose to the surface with wanting eyes. I was pleasantly surprised that it had not hurt a bit, pressing the needle into my arm. Again, I had never done this before so I was a little bit shaky. I pulled back a little direct hit, a splurge of red blood entered the device, and as I pushed in the plunger I knew there was no going back. I emptied the whole syringe into my arm. Pulling the needle out of my arm pinched a little, a small bead of blood rose to the surface, which I sucked off, and the taste of my blood irony, with a hint of pungent medication. I let the necktie fall to the floor and in an instant it had shown its face.

Now I do not know what you have been told. Movies overdue and overact the whole rush. What I can tell you is this. The warmth flooded my whole body. Euphoria like, I had never experienced this. I almost felt as though I was floating. Everything became very soft and placid; my mind swirled with colors and stars. It was amazing, truly amazing. I had to sit down. If not, I may have just fallen down. I made my way to the couch and slumped down like a sack of potatoes. It was like winning the Lotto, the first time being laid, or winning the gold medal, all at the same time. My eyes became like lead weights as I drifted off into another time and place—drifting, drifting, drifting, drifting away.

Just like that. My life began to tumble down into a downward spiral, a relentless pursuit into addiction, crime, mistrust, turmoil, confusion, hate and resentment. I really do not think there are enough nasty or descriptive words to explain what the next years would be like. In between, I would have moments of clarity. None of those would last long. For the most part, my days would be based on the getting and using heroin.

That sweet Chiba, horse, John, dope, Paul P Funk, whatever other name it has been called throughout the years. Songs have been written, poems, tales, and books. None like this, for this is my story and my path to destruction I left in my way.

When my running partner returned home, he was not surprised to see me in the state I was in. I was moving in a slow and rhythmic fashion. His surprise came when he entered the bathroom only to find the evidence left behind. In my stupor I had left behind a trail of evidence that needed neither investigation nor explanation.

"Holy shit, did you shoot yourself up? Where did you get the needle, where did you get the balls?"

I suffered a barrage of questions that at this point I was too high and really did not care to answer. My only out was to offer him the same taste.

"Here I grabbed this for you," I said, reaching into my pocket pulling out the other syringe.

His eyes opened wide and his lips turned up in an almost-smile. In his sarcastic, almost demeaning way, he said, "I knew you were good for something," and retreated to the bathroom to fix himself with this powdered evil.

By now, we were both regularly shooting dope. A daily activity, that took on as much importance as brushing your teeth and combing your hair. People are noticing a change in me everywhere I went. Something just screamed wrong, out of place.

At work, more than once, I was asked, "Are you alright?" due to the black circles under my eyes. See, when you use dope, you do not really sleep. You go into a sleep-like state. However, as far as sleeping, you just nod off. You never get the restful sleep your body needs.

Second, on more than one occasion, I came to work high, and I just looked a mess. Falling asleep while standing, eyes opens, looking like a fucking zombie. A creature out of a bad living-dead flick. In my mind, I looked completely normal and together. All was well. Trust me, truth was I was not well at all. Every other thing in my life took a backseat to my heroin use. My girlfriend was gone. School was everything but important; work was a time-killer place to go, and the money I needed to get high. My family, true friends, everything gone.

I remember one day in particular, my running partner and I went down to a bar. This was a brewery that we used to go. B, my true best friend and brother, bartended there. This particular night he had off, so we went down to shoot some darts and chill. Of course, my running partner and I are high, and now B, who happened to be there, is not stupid. He knew we were messing around with the stuff for a while, and I think he started to catch on to how bad it was getting. That night he told us both to get it together. We looked like shit, and he could see that it was getting worse. That was one of those evenings, I will never forget. That was the night where all of what you are trying to hide makes its way to the surface. Hot, like a lava burning everyone around you, and you yourself.

As I am writing this, I am doing my best to keep things in chronological order. Up until this point, my using was what I thought, a fad, a phase, so to speak. I still bullshitted myself that I could stop when I wanted. When I tried, it never lasted long. First, I would get uncomfortable and my skin would feel clammy. Next, the cold sweats, and then the hot sweats. Then the nausea and the shits. I mean, I would fall apart. What was happening? I have heard people talk about dope, sickness, but this was ridiculous. When I shot that special potion in me, all would cease and the cure became elegant and welcoming but I was again on this crazy coaster. I was riding; something would derail me off the track.

One day my running partner could not get in touch with our man. Frantic calls were made in order to reach him to no avail. The sickness began to show its evil eyes on both of us, and we knew it was time to do something.

I never asked how he met them but this would be around the time I would meet "John" and "Steph." They were married and had a child, a little girl. They were a bit dirty. They lived with John's mom, and they had access to dope. The problem was the process. See, they used and were the first real get-high dealers I had met. My running partner had called them and made the arrangements. I drove.

They lived in a nice little modest house. We arrived, knocked at the door and it opened and there is, John, tall, dark hair, super raspy voice, almost fake-sounding, like a cartoon character of some sort. Track marks that ran the length of his arm and his eyes with a permanent gray haze. My running partner introduced us, and we went upstairs. The air was thick with the smell of must, dust, and smoke. The bedroom we entered even worse. Dirty and unkempt. The bedspread resembled a connect-a-dot, for it was littered with burns from nodding and doping.

I would know this myself, all too soon. Trash TV showing on the small TV, a mangy couch littered with stains of who knows what substances, and of course Steph, the one that we would all come to love to hate. She was loud and said everything in a whiny voice. Not ugly but out of shape, but not too bad. I guess they became our connections, and for a very long time.

Problem was If you wanted a bag you had to get them one, so if you wanted one, it cost you 50 bucks. Bags were $25 apiece in our neck of the woods. More often than not, if you wanted more than one, she would whine at you to give them two. This became an extremely expensive habit for us. No longer did I need my running partner to cop dope. I could call her myself. This made things easier and harder. I can honestly say that although they were not people I would have normally associated with … there was a lingering friendship there. They burned me more than once, but in the friendliest way.

I met many people through John and Steph. Out of the 10 or so I had met, more than half of them are dead. Overdose is a bitch man. You have no clue. It is calming, and what it does is it runs you down like a freight train.

My car that I had at this time had finally kicked; the shock tower rotted out. One of those unexpected occurrences in life. I convinced my parents to let me take out a loan, which I did, and bought me a great car. Problem was, even though I was working and going to school, my habit was now becoming more demanding and expensive. I was doing my best to make ends meet. I was selling some weed on the side, which helped out, yet still I was finding it hard to make the bacon. I got the car. I am not sure how significant the cars were in the story yet, but soon, it was to have been put directly into the path of my destruction.

Okay, before I go much further, I must clarify a few things. I began to find pleasant sensations … as well [as] terror, when any opiate I could find, I would take. I would pop pills if someone had them. I would consult the ones I knew to be "street pharmacists" to see if they could be shot. If not, taken orally would do fine. I remember one time in particular a friend's stepfather had passed away of cancer. God rest his soul. He left behind a list of the accomplishments and people he had touched, as well as a huge bottle of liquid R. Now, for those of you who do not know, that is liquid morphine. Oh boy, did I go to work on that. I remember that being a particularly painful day for me as well. You see in those days, hypodermic needles could not be bought over the counter. So, a junkie like myself would use the needle to the point where it was so dull. It was like trying to puncture your skin with a spoon. That night, my friend "Jeff" and I went to a friend's house to hang out and play some music. Jeff and I have been friends 15 years, and we are still currently writing music with all the intentions to make it big.

I do not remember most of the evening. I do remember retreating to the car to fix myself again with the morphine solution. A short time later, after everyone wondered where I had disappeared to, I was found on the neighbor's porch passed out. I have no recollection whatsoever of how I got there.

So now I am popping pills and shooting anything I can liquefy into my veins, which are taking a beating from my dull syringe.

****

*Long-Sleeve Shirts*

Yes, that is right, the track marks. Ninety degrees in the summer, I'm the jerk-ass wearing long-sleeve shirts. I had long, scabby scars that just called out, "Hey, guess what we are. That's right, he's a junkie." Somewhere along the way, I developed the idea that only I could see those horrible god-awful tracks.

People are asking questions, not to me, but to each other, you know, comparing notes on my behavior and actions. Things were not right, but no one could put their finger on it. I returned to yet another attempt at school. The only class I really enjoyed was photography because it allowed me to express myself. I associated myself with the arts and therefore what I was doing to myself was part of what my art was.

One day, on returning to our apartment, I opened the door and there was my running partner sitting on the couch with his mother. Neither of their expressions were welcoming nor suggested I should have entered. I slowly crept out the door as I had come in and went to the photo lab in the basement of the art building not far from where I was. I liked it there—dark, alone, quiet, the smell of chemical. I soon found out via phone call to my running partner's girlfriend that he had told her what was going on. Specifically, that he and I were using heroin on a daily basis, and he felt it was getting out of hand. Fucker, he could have just told me. I mean, what the hell?

She, my running partner's girlfriend, contacted his mother, and told her he was moving back with [her], so she could take care of him. She, in a not-so-delicate way, told me to stay away from my running partner. The next day, the apartment was empty, and I was back with my parents. I told my mom and dad that things did work out for my running partner and his girlfriend, and they decided to give it another try, which meant me moving out.

I was barely, if at all, making ends meet now. How was I supposed to support an apartment? I am glad I did move home, though. Not long after I did, my grades arrived via mail. I was failing everything but photography. Not good at all! Not everything was bad, though. Around this time I had met a really cool chick who I had become very fond of, "Mary," a beauty with pigtails and a killer smile. Younger than me, but bright and talented. I loved hanging out with her. We hit it off the first day we met. I was listening to a bootleg tape first, live Terrapin, and pulled into a gas station in my little blue Beemer. There she was. She worked outside assisting customers. "Hey," she said, "nice tunes."

We talked, laughed, and made plans to hang out. I met many cool people. Some will reappear later in time. One in particular, "Jack," was one of many who would question and lecture me on my apparent drug use. Never did I know what the future would bring; none of us did. I knew I loved Mary; I knew Mary loved me. However, what she did not like was the heroin. I told you she was smart. It was at this point I realized neither did I.

The first time I totaled my car was a blur. I had finished classes and walked across the commons that were filled with laughter and the playing of whiffle ball. I thought to myself, I hate this stuff, heroin, what a great time I would be having if I was just one of those kids playing whiffle ball.

I had made my way to my friend's little on-campus room. I loved going there. It was an old Victorian house turned into school dorms. His room had particular character with its rooftop angels and ornate woodworking, just a great place to relax. This particular day, a kid who I had seen on campus but really did not know, was there, and we were listening to and smoking a joint. He also had the small blue pills he was more than happy to crush up and snort with me.

"What are these, valiums?" I asked.

"No man, Klonopin, super great downers. You'll love it."

"Is it going to annihilate me, though?" Knowing I had to drive.

"No, man, you will be fine, just spacey and chill."

Spacey and chill was a gross understatement of how I was about to feel. I left and quickly made my way to my car in hopes of getting to where I had to go before this railed me, if it was indeed going to. I wasn't sure what to expect due to I had never done this suspicious substance and I had shot a bag earlier that day. I flew down the highway to my pot dealer's house. This guy was a hoot; I knew him from high school, a year older than me.

Not a minute after pulling up, I could feel my eyes begin to feel weighted and heavy. My mind began to wander, my vision blurred. It was not a dopey feeling, though. It was very chemical, very uncertain, and a sensation of weightlessness. He knew something was wrong.

"Wow, what is up with you dude? You look like three sheets to the wind."

I explained the scenario earlier, how I had sniffed some shit.

"Never good to do nothing unless you know. Man, something like that could kill you."

Kill me? I was immortal. Nothing was going to kill me. I did what I had to and left.

I remember getting onto the highway. From that point, I remember nothing. Until bam! The sound of my poor little Beemer being eaten alive by the thick, steel guardrail was one I choose to never hear again and wish I never heard. Sparks flew from the passenger side, grinding metal. The engine whined, trying to keep the wheels spinning as my little "Dead Bee," affectionately named by Mary, bled her fluids onto the asphalt. My eyes were open, and really had blasted me like a 12-gauge to the chest. Holy shit! I knew the severity of what had happened, but I was so close. Please make it to the exit. Once on the exit, please make it to the gas station. That little car pulled and pushed with a scream. Bleeding the whole way but she made it. I pulled into the gas station. I have no clue how I made it. All I do know is that this completely reaffirmed my love of this car. I was hysterical, I was teetering on the verge of a nervous breakdown and a drug-induced coma. I called Mary that night. She was the only one I thought I could tell about what happened. She picked me up, called my parents, and explained I had been in an accident. Blown tire was the official ruling, at least that is what everyone else thought. I knew and a few others. Mary was my guardian angel that evening. She was a true friend. It was about this time that even she questioned me hard.

I still saw my running partner. I was getting high every day, in-between classes, even though I hated the stuff. I would go to my friend's and shoot up there. I carried my little kit with me everywhere I went in a sunglass case. Black leather, held a syringe, spoon, cotton ball, pack of matches, and a few loose bags perfectly. He didn't care that I was there; he was usually in such an acid stupor. I could have been a big purple elephant, and he wouldn't have known the difference.

My car was in the shop after the accident, I had it towed to a friend of my father's who said he could fix it, more than likely. It just would not be cheap; lack of transportation screwed things up a little. It made things a little more difficult. I borrowed my parents' car when needed to get back and forth to school or work. They knew something was up but never what was really happening.

Most of my crimes up until that point were petty. Small crimes to get by, a couple of bucks here, a couple bucks there. Stealing change from my parents, a few bucks off the dresser. My sister's babysitting money became target, always with the intention to pay it back. Any way to get what I needed without blowing off a whole can full of smoke to draw attention to what was going on. Things returned somewhat normal. My car had been repaired, although it didn't look as nice as it had, for it now had a black hood and fender, but it was somewhat back to normal and ran as well as it had.

I continued the charade of getting dope, shooting dope, getting dope, shooting dope. I was trying at school to get by but failing. I was trying to hide the fact that I was failing and failing. I made every attempt to look, act, and seem normal. Then it came. Like a blow to the chest by a heavyweight boxer. Like a direct hit from a freight train.

I had expected this would happen someday. I mean, how could I hide it forever? I arrived at work about 10 a.m., my normal time, greeted everyone, started my day like everyone there. I played a few games and set the party room up for a birthday party I had coming in at noon. No sooner did the clock hit 11, my manager approached me with a panicked expression.

She said, "Honey, your mom is on the phone, and she says it's an emergency."

I began to feel my heart pound, my sweat bead, and my blood boil. I ran to the phone. "Hello Mom, what's up?"

"Honey, Dad and I need you to come home. There's a family emergency," my mom said with a level of cool and caution in her voice. There was definitely something wrong.

"Mom, what the hell is going on? Is something wrong? Is Dad okay?"

"Everyone is okay. Just come home."

That is what I did. Everyone saw the panic on my face, knew something was terribly wrong.

"If you need to go, go. We are fine here. Just call me later. Let me know everything's okay."

I ran to my car with the speed of the Jaguar and drove home just as fast. Rounding the corner to my house, I saw my friend's truck outside. He was one of my oldest childhood friends and neighbors. He had recently moved in with his girlfriend … Incidentally, he is married now and with children. If his truck was there, something terrible must have happened. What could it be? My heart raced. I mentally prepared myself for the worst of situations, a death, a stroke, a terrible accident, but I had not prepared myself for what happened next.

That is where his writing ends, and that was the day I found out that my son was a heroin addict.

# I Become Enlightened

My son's girlfriend stopped by our house on the evening of February 20, 2012. She did not look well at all, but I probably looked worse. She asked if she could go up into his room one last time. I said yes. I sat downstairs staring at the television while she went upstairs. She came down shortly thereafter with a couple of personal items and papers that she needed. It was a quick visit, and I really was not sure why she was there.

That Wednesday, February 22, the girl's sister called me and said that she had relapsed over the weekend. The sister wanted to know where my son's last running partner lived because she suspected my son's girlfriend was with him. I gave her directions to his house while she was driving, and she found her sister's car.

The next day, I texted my son's last running partner. I asked him about my son's girlfriend. He could tell that I did not know.

He wrote, "I'm sorry, Mrs. Marks, I didn't realize that you didn't know she was an addict."

He told me that the two of them had relapsed around March 2011; at least that was what he remembered. What a fool I was!

She was not in a mental-health facility when she was supposed to be cat sitting with my son. She was in detox, while my son was at my sister-in-law's house. His running partner was with him the whole time, and they had convinced themselves they would get clean once and for all. My son's friend hid in the backyard when my brother-in-law stopped by to check on my son. His friend told me that my husband had left a message on our son's cell phone telling him he knew about the credit-card charges. My son was fully aware of what he would face that Friday at court. His friend told me that he was there at the house with my son until that Thursday. It was that Thursday night, almost Friday morning, that my son took his own life. His friend had no idea that he was contemplating suicide.

On February 24, his girlfriend's sister came to our house to drop off the phone. She felt very sad that our son had died, and I could tell her feelings were genuine. She started to explain that her sister used to be a "nice" girl. She did not need to explain how a nice person could become an addict. I already knew that. She told us the reason her sister did not have a phone was because her mother had it shut off, and that is why her mother wanted us to take the phone back. No wonder her mother asked me if I loved her and acted so surprised when I said, yes. No wonder they kept such a close eye on her at the funeral. They knew what was going on and probably thought I did too. They must have thought I was a crazy person for letting this continue. I honestly did not know that she was using. Shame on me!

I talked about the day they were moving out of her apartment and had to go to the store and get some containers. I mentioned that she walked into our house crying because he had been picked up on a bench warrant. Well, that was not true either. After we cleaned his room just this past February 2014, I found the arrest ticket. My son was actually arrested for shoplifting that day, not a bench warrant. I know drug addicts cover for each other, which is part of their disease, but I wish she had told us about the trouble at her Christmas party and all the other problems. I may have realized how bad it had gotten for him. I had become so immune. Her sister did not know about the incident at the Christmas party until the day she dropped off the phone. I guess everything was a surprise to everybody—the kind of surprises you do not want.

Just to review the facts: She was not in a mental-health ward; she was at detox. She did not have her phone turned off; her mother took it away from her. She never went to rehab during the summer of 2010; she was at detox. We are talking about the difference of four to five days as opposed to maybe twenty-eight. A friend who knew her then told me this. That is why she could not pay her bills anymore. Even the seasoned parent can be fooled.

Now I "get" it. If he was responsible for her relapse, or whatever the case may be, he could not accept that responsibility anymore. He was a good actor, but I do not think he had it in him anymore.

# EPIDEMIC

One of the major news channels in our area had a whole series recently on heroin addiction, including where addicts can go for help and counselors staffing the phones. They were running it like a telethon. From what I have learned, I do not think that will work, but at least they are trying. Every channel I turn to, I see people talking about heroin addiction and how it affects our children. Now they are starting to reach out and help these people. I guess my son was born at the wrong time.

Since his death, it seems everyone talks about addiction as if it were a startling, new problem. Every news channel, every newspaper, every entertainment show reports almost daily on the epidemic of addiction. However, this is not a new problem. Sometimes I resent the fact that some high-profile people had to die before we realized we have a true crisis on our hands. This stuff has been creeping into our neighborhoods and schools for a long time, and I ask myself, *Why now, after my son's death?* They even call a highway that connects a local town with a nearby state the Heroin Highway. How sad.

The governor of a nearby state called a press conference to discuss the epidemic of heroin in high schools. Empty bags of heroin had been found strewn in the halls. Recently, there was an article in the paper about a boy in a high school just north of us who was caught "shooting up" a girl with heroin in a school bathroom.

The fact that addiction has become an epidemic is an understatement. This is not new.

# FAITH

A few months after my son died, I called the priest who gave the eulogy at his wake. I needed to talk to somebody who might understand how I was feeling about my religion. I had begun to question my faith over the years.

The priest asked me, "Are you mad at God?"

I could not bring myself to say yes. What I did say was, "Well, Father, I did an awful lot of praying." I guess that was an indirect way of answering his question. I often felt that my prayers were not answered. The praying for my son's recovery and sobriety was constant.

The priest said one thing to me that I often repeat to myself: "Find peace in His peace." That is my new mantra. It is the only thing that makes sense to me. His peace!

I had also been seeing a counselor and would talk to her about my despair over losing my son. One time I told her that I felt very guilty that our bad behavior as young parents may have prompted my son to become an addict.

She looked at me with a smile on her face and said kindly, "Your bad behavior as a young person did not do this to him. Yes, he might have acted out, but your son acquired the gene of addiction."

I thought to myself, *Yes, she is right.* That is what happened; he acquired the gene of addiction. I think addicts struggle with a deep pain of want. With addiction, that want is for something that is not good for them and strips their souls. They go through stages with their addiction that can lead to rock bottom, and for some, rock bottom is death.

Every time I open up the obituaries, I recognize them. They are usually young people in their thirties or even early twenties, men and women who just happened to die suddenly. It does not take a brain surgeon to understand. I was reading the obituaries one morning and saw an item about a young woman. She was beautiful, she was talented, and they described her as loving, compassionate, and very well liked. I certainly never doubted what those parents had to say about their daughter. I knew what they were going through because I had experienced their nightmare. Her parents had the courage, as we did, to say that she died from the disease of addiction.

# Epilogue

It is now January 20, 2015. The third year since my son's death. I have been over what I have written thirty times. Each time I read it and realize how trite it all sounds.

Finding peace in His peace has been difficult for me. My main objective for sixteen years was to catch my son in the net I had carried around with me for so many years. For me, there is still a lot of reprogramming to do. Remember, I was addicted to the addict. My drug is gone. My husband has finally gotten to the point where he realizes that my son was a very sick young man and had a terrible disease. Hallelujah.

My husband is a completely different man than he was when my son was alive. My son would be very proud of him. He apologized for not treating me well during our marriage. He realizes now that he was very hard on our son. Yes, he was.

My son is someone I will always miss. I am not as patient and loving as I used to be. I honestly do not know how I am not crazy. I pretty much stay to myself, and I have written many people out of my life. I just do not want the drama anymore. I still work, and I have to admit that if it were not for my wonderful coworkers and the doctors, I probably would not be alive today. Some very wonderful people have stood by my side through my grief, and I thank them tremendously.

My daughter gave birth to my beautiful grandson on June 30, 2014, just one day after my son's birthday. He is a delight, and his uncle would have loved him very much. My son loved children.

****

What happened to my relationship with my sister? She did try to reconnect with me, and I tried too. She used to come over my house, sit with me, and listen to me cry. She tried to comfort me with her words, stating that she did not let my son's heroin addiction define him. I certainly appreciated her words.

This went on for months. She never apologized to me about the incidents following the deaths of our parents. She never apologized for leaving me feeling totally alienated. It was never discussed. I never knew if she realized how hurt I was by that entire scenario. I never really grieved properly for my mother and father. None of my family did.

My sister bought the plaque for my son's cemetery plot; for that I am grateful, and I wanted her to be aware of that fact. We did not have the money, and she offered.

As time went on, I found that my sister made me cry every time she came over. There was nothing comforting about her visits. She talked to me like I was a child. I sent her a letter stating that I could no longer pretend nothing had happened. I did not trust her and could not build up the trust again. For the sake of my own sanity, I had to let go.

I also thought that everything that happened after my parents' death had a very bad effect on my children. They both were made to feel unimportant in my mother and father's lives. I learned recently that my son had discussed this with a close friend, and he felt a lot of guilt about the way my family treated me. He and I never discussed it, but I know it hurt him.

My husband came home one day and told me he had stopped by the place where our son used to work. Two of the young men there told my husband that they had been meaning to stop by and apologize. I guess because of the way they treated him when he relapsed. They said they were "ashamed of the way they had treated" our son. If I told you how many of his friends have told me, "if only I had known then what I know now, I would have done things so differently." All I can hope is that people do realize that good souls do become addicts.

There is a reason I did not approach my in-laws about my son staying at their house to watch the cat, why I did not call them myself. The simple explanation is that after years in which our lives were so chaotic—dealing with my son in this world of addiction—I could not stand the chaos anymore. Additional drama was not something I needed in my life.

There were a number of incidents where both my in-laws had too much to drink. Believe me, I get it, we all make mistakes, but one night she came over to our house and stood at the foot of my bed, telling me how her husband was a rotten alcoholic. Then her husband came barreling into our house, walked into the room, and started arguing with her at the foot of my bed. Really? I could have handled that, but the next episode did me in.

She called her brother, my husband, and told him she had called the police because her husband "tried to run her over with the car in the driveway." She asked my husband to please pick her up, and take her to our house. We drove over to her house, a short distance from our own. In the driveway stood her husband backed up against a car with his arms folded, and two policemen standing there, protecting her until my husband escorted her to our car. As my husband walked by him, my brother-in-law said, "You're going to get yours." We took her to our house, and she cried and told us she was going to get a lawyer and start divorce proceedings. I knew it was just drunk talk. I had been there and seen this scene before.

That entire summer, she went to parties with us and told everyone that she was getting a divorce. People would ask me if it were true. Now she is back with her husband again, and she wonders why her brother does not particularly care for him. Well, go figure. I had enough. I never made it public or family knowledge that my husband and I were having problems. It was our problem, not theirs, and I tried very hard not to taint my parents against my husband.

One afternoon I called my mother-in-law when my husband was staying with his mother, sister, and brother, and I was alone with the kids at our house. His sister answered the phone, and when I asked if I could speak with my husband, she said, "No, I'm sorry, he's eating." I had known her since she was twelve years old. She should have told her brother to get up and speak to his wife. I was done. I needed to choose my battles.

I never discussed my feelings about her with my son. I believed my son could be friends with his aunt and uncle; they were his family. That was just natural to me, but it was my decision to back off, and that is what I did. I tried very hard not to sway family members one way or the other. I expected the same treatment, which is why, unfortunately, they were not aware that my son had relapsed. I do not blame her for my son's death, although that is what she tells people. That was on him.

****

When my son relapsed and lost everything in 2009, it was not a matter of me keeping him clean anymore. It was a matter of me trying to keep him alive. My son had to keep himself clean. I could not do that for him. Keeping him alive was my main goal, and I know that now more than ever.

I have papers strewn all over the table—arrest records, emergency-room visits, refusals from detox, all sorts of things that just bring back terrible memories. There are times when I wonder if my son was put here to teach us things. God knows I know more about life. Maybe that was his journey. If one person in some way is helped, then his life will be for something.

I came across one thing while I was looking through all those papers. I found the obituary comments that we printed after he died, and there is one I would like to share. It is from a young woman who went to high school with my son. If you had known him, you would have felt the same way. My son graduated in 1995. She wrote:

> When [we] heard about _____ passing, it shocked many of his fellow high school classmates. He was friends with many, and many of us remember him

fondly as the funny one. I was a graduate in 1994 and will always remember that he was one of the few who was liked by all, simply because he was an all-around nice person. I will always remember him as the nice guy that made me smile. He has touched many, and now I live in _____ so now we can say that he has touched the world.

# MY DEAR SON

My beautiful son, I am glad that you are no longer wandering the streets trying to score dope. This is not how I hoped your addiction would end. As they say, it is what it is. Guess what? I have finally stopped smoking cigarettes. I will always love and miss you. This is your book. I will try to find peace in your peace.

Until then,
Mom

# Addition

At first, I was not quite sure what to do with his request to "not let his life be for nothing." Then I decided I would write the book he should have written himself. It will never be close to what he could have written but I will do my best.

*Maybe,* I thought, *someday, somewhere, one person will read it and benefit from his experience.* This book may shed new light for you. I hope you will understand that addiction is not a life of self-indulgence but a life of self-destruction.

# About the Author

Born in New York City in 1952, when life seemed simpler and without the complexities of our new world, B. L. Marks is a nurse who has worked in the ob-gyn field for more than thirty years. She had a beautiful son and daughter. She and her husband worked very hard to keep their young and tumultuous marriage together. It is not true what they say; people do change. Both she and her husband succeeded in having a marriage that worked. That was what she was taught to do: make it work.

She went to parochial schools in the 1960s and felt that the wrath of God came down on her when her beautiful son became a heroin addict. In spite of all her tragedy, she finds great joy in her beautiful daughter and her first grandchild. She regrets that her son will never know this child because he would have loved him immensely. She is stronger than she thought she was. Now, she wants to change how society approaches the treatment and recovery of addicts.

Printed in the United States
By Bookmasters